BREAD & BUTTER

BREAD & BUTTER

History, Culture, Recipes

Richard Snapes, Grant Harrington
& Eve Hemingway

Photography by Patricia Niven

quadrille

Introduction

There are few pairings eaten so frequently as bread and butter, and even fewer so entrenched in such a variety of global cultures. It's hard to think of other food double acts that are as inseparable. Would salt and pepper count? Is seasoning substantial enough to go head-to-head with bread and butter? Other pairings may complement each other perfectly – think pea and mint, beef and horseradish, tomato and basil, ham and mustard – but none of them create quite the same 'ah-ha' moment as bread and butter.

Perhaps it's because bread and butter have been eaten for such a long time. Although, let's be clear, humans were eating bread some 10,000 years before they were eating butter. It then took another 10,000 years for them to be eaten together (or at least until we have material evidence). How it took so long to arrive at this delicious pairing is beyond us, but if we have learnt anything from bread and butter's 20,000 year history, it's that they really do seem to exist in some form no matter where you are from… and they are, blessedly, going nowhere.

The reason

Why write a book about bread and butter? What makes such a humble pairing, and ostensibly a minor event of the day, become a heroic match worthy of exploration over 256 pages?

Well, if you're reading this, you probably quite like bread and butter and you've probably liked it for some time. You might remember it as a childhood treat – simple for a parent to slice, spread and share to keep you quiet. Perhaps, when under the weather, you note the heartening feeling of spying a doorstop slice thick with golden spread, precariously balanced at the edge of a bowl of steaming soup. Maybe you're responsible for prepping the sandwiches, making sure so-and-so's has no crusts, and heaven forbid the tomato makes the bread soggy. You might be a regular toast-eater, your tongue swiftly following yellow rivers of butter dripping down your wrist after impatient morning crunches. You could, in other words, be deeply in love with bread and butter, and yet know very little about it.

When we looked at other cookbooks on the shelves, we saw turquoises, fuchsias and golds promising titillation of the senses from cultures unknown to us. Alongside these exotic titles, there were beaming faces, promising ways to improve your gut health, even change your microbiome. And, delving deeper, books for the real food nerds, the ones that really make you think about how and why we eat what we eat.

At first we couldn't see how bread and butter, two such quotidian foodstuffs, could stand up to these vibrant and exotic subjects. Surely, they could not transport you beyond the familiar, or aid digestion or teach you something you didn't know because: you eat them every day. Or most days at least. Yet, on reflection, we realised that bread and butter can do all of these things.

Bread and butter exists in weird and wonderful forms across the world, making them truly global products. Between us, we've seen a Tibetan cream separator that looks more like an intricate jewellery box, its mahogany lacquer and polished brass dials emanating pride and expertise. In the Polish celebration of *nowe latko*, literally meaning 'new summer' but celebrated at the end of the year, bread figurines of a man with a bobble cap surrounded by eight geese are made to encourage abundance in the fields in the coming year. And in Amarante in Portugal, the *bolos de São Gonçalo* (Saint Gonçalo cakes) are phallic-shaped breads or, more commonly now, pastries, intricately iced and given to single women as lucky love charms. We're sure the recipients are very, um, grateful.

With regard to health, we cannot promise our dishes will do wonders for your waistline (many of these recipes are a far cry from cauliflower rice and cashew cheese), but well-being also comes from pleasure. The Danish, for example, have an apt, joy-filled phrase, *tandsmør*, meaning 'tooth butter', to describe the teeth marks you leave in butter when it's spread thickly enough on bread. It is this generosity of spirit we love and hope you will find here.

And in terms of teaching you something, we swiftly recognised the wealth of information and experience we three authors could share. From the origins and history of bread and butter, via the science, and on to a passionate appreciation of the resurgence of interest in bread and butter crafted with care. As demand is showing, people are ready for something a little different, even if it takes longer, looks wonky or varies slightly from batch to batch. Flavour is the most important thing.

This book is a celebration, a love letter and a record of bread and butter: it adores them and reveals their mysteries; it unpacks their history and champions their future.

The authors

Richard founded The Snapery Bakery and supplies some of the best restaurants in London with sourdough bread and buns. Grant founded Ampersand Bulture Culture, and makes cultured butter among other dairy-related products, which are also served in Michelin-starred restaurants across the UK. Their philosophies are similar – both have a focus on slow, fermented products, which are delicious alone and even better together.

They met selling their wares on Druid Street Market in South London. Their stalls were put next to each other, Richard selling his bread and Grant selling his butter. Before long they bonded over the tables and joined forces, selling their products together, tag-teaming between running the stall and picking up beers from nearby brewers. I joined in when I had spare time, learning a lot and eating a lot in the process.

These days the stall is at the equally brilliant Maltby Street Market, but we all still enjoy that gentle hum of weekend market life, talking to other traders and nibbling on buttery morsels meant for market-goers. All the early mornings, late nights, tears, sweat and Birkenstocks are somehow worth it.

The structure

The first third of the book covers history and culture, while the latter two-thirds are filled with tempting recipes. We want the book to be something you can dip in and out of, or sit with for an afternoon, with a slice of bread and butter to snack on, of course.

Through the rich and delicious history of bread and butter, we look at where it all began and how we came to eat bread and butter in the first place. We travel through the Fertile Crescent, Rome and Greece and explore centuries of history. We look at how and why the popularity of bread and butter accelerated massively from 1500s onwards, and touch on the agricultural and industrial techniques that caused these products to shift and change as speed and scale were prioritised over flavour. Finally, we look at the resurgence of bread and butter. For some time now, there has been a rekindling of less efficient methods that produce quite different breads and butters – ones that are a little less predictable and much more flavoursome.

To do bread and butter justice, we wanted to look beyond cookbooks, and beyond the Western European traditions familiar to the three of us – so the culture section romps through the many wonderful and delicious breads and butters enjoyed around the world.

The recipes, meanwhile, cover four areas: bread, butter, bread and butter, and leftovers. We have deliberately included recipes for making bread and butter from scratch, as well as recipes that use bread and butter as ingredients, in order to suit the keen, time-poor and every cook in between. Many of the recipes do take quite a bit of preparation and some need special equipment.

Equally, there are some that can be whipped up in less than half an hour. We've tried to cater for a variety of tastes and skill sets as we know not everyone has whole weekends at their disposal. Regarding the last chapter, the three of us are passionate anti-food-waste advocates and want to encourage you to use up all those old bits of leftover bread and buttermilk in inventive ways.

We are so excited to share this book with you, and grateful to have been given such free rein to explore two foods we're sure many take for granted, and to re-examine them not just through recipes, but through their history and culture. We hope you enjoy our findings as much as we have enjoyed the discoveries.

Richard, Grant & Eve

Natural bread is digestible, delicious and makes a damn good sandwich.

Richard Snapes

I grew up in village in Northamptonshire. There was a pub and a local shop… then the shop closed down because there weren't enough people to support it, that's how small it was. One of the only things to do was explore: nature was a huge part of our lives and we didn't know much beyond its realm.

The fields were very important to us as children, for one reason: hay bale dens. As anyone who grew up in a rural area will know, building a den is the pinnacle of a kid's summer. There is no

den greater than a bale fort – and my brother's were the best in Northamptonshire!

My dad was often on our allotment, which was between our garden and the fields. After playing I'd stop and chat to my dad and see what was growing. He'd send me back to the house with veg for mum. Having grown up with organic vegetables that were picked and cooked within minutes, nothing shop bought has ever come close. This simplicity has stuck with me, and is still part of my cooking and baking today.

My first memory of real bread comes from my grandparents. They'd cook an incredible roast in the Aga, with a bowl of dough proving by the side of the huge oven. Intensely wheaty, this 100% wholemeal loaf was a real treat sliced as thinly as possible and topped with a lot of good butter. I can still remember the slightly sweet and savoury taste. Baking bread was just a normal thing for them to do.

Outside of home life, I was an awful student. Most of my day was spent with my head in the clouds, which meant I turned my attention to music. From the age of 19 I pursued a career in music while working jobs I was willing to quit in an instant if I was needed to play a show. The more focus I put on music, the less work I would find, the more underemployed I became. Eventually I had to go back to my home village, broke. I decided that to earn my keep I would cook every day for my parents, working through various cookbooks and gaining knowledge and skill week on week.

After a year or so I'd become good enough to apply for a job at a gastropub in Northampton. The chef, Brett Rollings, took a chance on me. It wasn't an easy ride. Years of freedom, music and home cooking meant I had no grasp of structure. Brett was incredibly patient and stuck with me… I had my moments!

Following a move to London I was still working in kitchens and playing music. But both take the same amount of commitment. It's almost impossible for them to co-exist. I remember at least two incidents in the kitchen after band tours where I had to go to hospital after slicing myself due to overtiredness.

Soon after, I bought a copy of *Crust* by Richard Bertinet, and like my days as a personal chef to my parents, I applied myself to it.

Utterly inspired by the nature of sourdough I was compelled to bake at every opportunity. Another new passion… but this was different. I felt a connection with the simplicity of the ingredients, and a link to my days in the fields, and with my grandparents' home baking. When the dough was mixed, I could smell the wheat, and it reminded me of home.

After many friends told me I should do something with my new-found skill, I finally got the nerve to make the decision that would change my life. I quit everything to start The Snapery Bakery. I worked almost on my own for 6 months, without a day off in a space I found in Bermondsey. I would sleep with my head on the mixer. I worked 18-hour days. It had gone from liking, to loving, to obsession. Inbetween moments of sheer panic I started to build a customer base by turning up unannounced at restaurant kitchen doors with bread. The strategy worked and with some newly enlisted baker on board, we sought a larger space. After another 12 months we were supplying Bermondsey's best restaurants. With a strong team, we were ready to rock. And we've been rocking ever since.

Bread is a simple joy – everyone can make it given a little knowledge. The process is easy, but there will be slight variants that make each loaf different. The anticipation of opening the oven to see your loaf for the first time is one that I still feel every day. After baking hundreds of thousands of loaves, that feeling remains.

You might feel happy, sad, confused, indifferent or amused. It's this that makes our jobs so interesting. I could make one type of bread every day for the rest of my life and still find excitement, wonderment and delight in the smell of those first baked loaves in the early hours of the morning. **RS**

I created Ampersand Butter Culture with the sole aim of making butter taste as buttery as I possibly could.

Grant Harrington

It was my time as a cook in kitchens across Europe that led to my eventual devotion to butter. During an intense couple of years in London working under Gordon Ramsay, I learnt a lot about the importance of a good work ethic, as well as just how much butter it is possible to put into a sauce (it turns out it is an outrageous amount, and it makes *everything* taste better!). For me, 17-hour days charging around a hot, windowless kitchen was a turning point. As I worked through the ranks of a chef, I began to define myself as a cook who first and foremost valued the importance of ingredients, and this, in turn, led me to Fäviken in Sweden to work under Magnus Nilsson.

At Fäviken every ingredient is scrutinised: it always needs to be the very best it can be. I already knew that vegetables could be grown and stored with the sort of respect that results in the most delicious outcome, and from Magnus I understood that meat could be aged to intensify its 'meatiness'. But the heights that the simple, staple ingredient butter could reach was an absolute revelation. I tried the butter on my first day on the job and literally did a double take – the flavour just blew me away, and it inspired me to pursue this butter-making path.

I learnt a lot about the traditional and ancient techniques that produce this more flavourful, buttery butter in Sweden, and back home I spent a year researching dairy fermentation and butter, with a focus on the science of lactic cultures. It was around this time my brother got married (coincidentally to a dairy farmer's daughter!) on a small dairy farm in Oxfordshire. I was honoured to cater: seven extravagant whole sirloins spit-roasted, and stem ginger and chocolate raw milkshakes for 150 people, but it was the butter everyone commented on and remembered. A sundried tomato butter (the recipe is on page 154) and a simple salted cultured butter were the standout hits.

So I took the obvious next step: with the help of my uncle, I built and installed a cabin on that same dairy farm and started making butter by hand (a process I still use to this day). Pretty soon I was making butter I felt confident with, and I started supplying local gastropubs. This led to other customers, including some 20 Michelin-starred restaurants, such as Bibendum, Restaurant Sat Bains and Le Manoir aux Quat'Saisons. Shops were also keen on the butter, like Fortnum & Mason and Harrods.

It seemed there was, and continues to be, a real demand for butter that is fresh, crafted carefully and made using top-quality ingredients (milk produced from English-bred Jersey dairy cows, a healthy culture and a touch of Himalayan sea salt). And I'm delighted to see such a staple, delicious and important ingredient being recognised globally for its significance on the dinner table. **GH**

Part of the joy in mastering the making of good bread and butter is that no matter how expert you become, you are still somewhat at their mercy.

Eve Hemingway

I'm not sure I can call myself a food writer, but I have wanted to write about food for as long as I can remember. Luckily I got to know Grant through Rich when Druid Street Market in South London was still going. I helped out on the market stall and probably snacked on more of the samples than I'd care to admit. I love their products, so when they asked if I'd write a book with them, I was more than happy to oblige.

Grant and Rich are two producers who have heavily influenced how I think about food. Sustainable, tasty, high-calorie produce is my passion, so I'm a great fan of their work. But it's not all about eating: I'm a food nerd and am equally interested in production methods as I am about taste. From its inception through to digestion, I love learning about food, and feel lucky to be part of a generation that is excited to find out as much as possible about what's on our plates and how it got there.

In my teens, I was given Delia's *How to Cook* (parts I, II and III) and methodically worked my way through all the volumes, learning to boil eggs, fry onions and bake bread. For my 16th birthday, I went to watch cookery writer Sophie Grigson in our local village hall stew oranges with black peppercorns. Though, it seems, I was on a food-focused path long before this.

Apparently, aged four, sitting at the dinner table, I would pause half-way through my main course, tilt my head to one side and sincerely ask, 'pudding?'. Patience has never been a strong point, and I still need to walk out of the kitchen after baking to allow bread and cakes to cool before tearing into them.

Memories of pudding are undoubtedly important, but it's an earlier memory that must have informed so much of how I think about food today. I remember being a small child and putting cake ingredients in a stand mixer. A tea towel would be draped over the top of the mixer so the flour wouldn't cover the kitchen in its dust. Mum would turn the mixer on to a slow setting, pick me up and we'd periodically peek under the tea towel to see if the mixture was ready to be poured into the tin. We would alternate between chatting and peeking, chatting and peeking. There was something about this process that took time and care in equal measure. Not rushing and letting the food do its good work.

I hope I've managed to capture a little of that care and joy in my recipes, and I hope the background history and culture offer a chance to reflect on two truly outstanding ingredients. **EH**

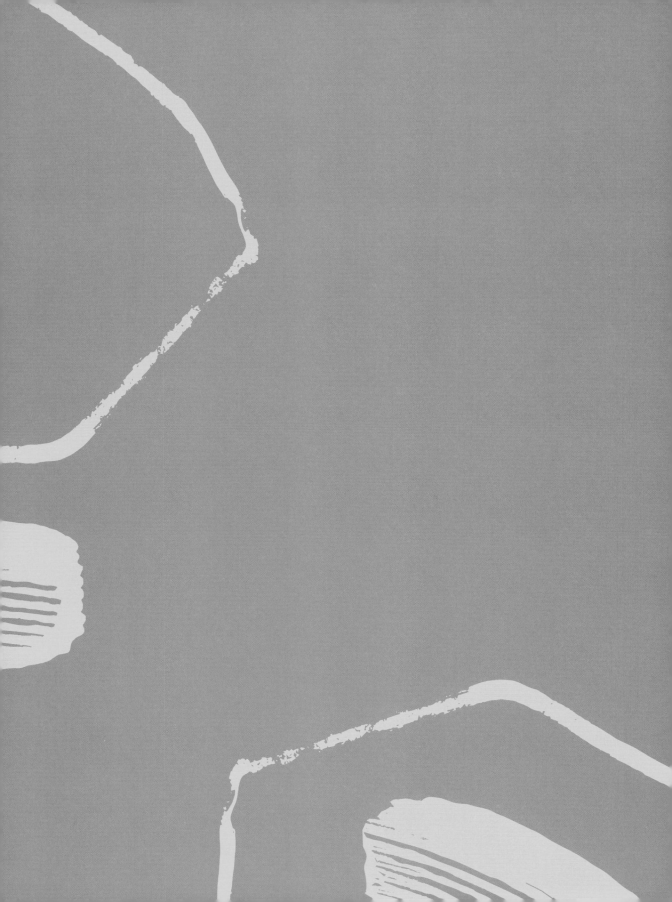

HISTORY
&
CULTURE

Ancient origins

In this chapter we look at how people came to make and eat bread and butter in the first place. What follows is by no means a comprehensive account, but rather a compilation of the elements we found most scintillating, charting the origins of bread, followed by butter… and then, yes, both together.

Origins of bread

Let's begin with the humble loaf – and it's useful to understand exactly what this is before we move on. The Oxford English Dictionary defines bread as 'A well-known article of food prepared by moistening, kneading and baking meal or flour, generally with the addition of yeast or leaven'. And when we talk about sourdough, we mean bread made solely with flour from grains (as opposed to legumes and pulses), plus salt, water and a cultured starter.

So when did it all begin? To find out, we turned to the mighty font of all knowledge, the British Library. We started at the turn of the twentieth century and with John Ashton, a little known yet prolific literary antiquarian, who wrote *The History of Bread: From Pre-historic to Modern Times* (circa 1904). Ashton was thorough and diligent in his research (as he was with his other texts on gossip, gambling and zoology), and he combed through archaeological texts for records of early tools and vessels used to grind or store grain. In referencing digs near lakes in Switzerland, however, Ashton doesn't narrow down the time frame for the origins of bread to any more narrower than 'pre-historic' – which, considering the Stone Age spans 3.4 million years, is not the most helpful.

History teaches us that trying to be too specific when looking this far back will likely be fruitless, but surely we could do a little better. We went directly to Ashton's source, scanning Dr Oswald Heer's *Treatise on the Plants of the Lake Dwellings* (1866), only to find the following: 'With respect to the age of the early settlements of this nature [where grain and grain-grinding tools had been found], we have not a single safe datum to guide our determination, so that it is quite impossible with any probability to decide even approximately the century or the centuries when they existed.' Which has to be the longest way of saying 'we don't know' that we've ever come across. The author's best guess is sometime during the Iron or Bronze Ages, going by some metal tools found at the site. Not entirely satisfied with this answer either, we continued our search.

We had hopes for *Six Thousand Years of Bread: Its Holy and Unholy History,* written by Heinrich Eduard Jacob and first published shortly after World War II. The clue was surely in the title! The book itself is a roller-coaster ride of anecdotes, at times somewhat tentatively, yet enjoyably, tied to bread. By way of an example, the opening story tells of Darwin presenting a correspondence between himself and a Texan professor on whether ants invented agriculture (we'll just leave that one with you for a moment). In the section on pre-historic bread, Jacob acknowledges evidence of grains and grain cultivation dating 15,000 years, but claims that Egyptians were the first to make bread, approximately 6000 years ago. This would pre-date both the Iron and Bronze Ages, throwing Dr Heer's assumptions out of the window – and further complicating our research.

Never ones to be easily deterred, we ploughed on. It was only when reading William Rubel's *Bread: A Global History* (2015) that we chanced upon what we were looking for. An archaeological dig at a site named Ohalo II, in the Fertile Crescent near the Sea of Galilee, revealed starch from barley and einkorn on a stone tool used for grinding grains about 22,500 years ago. Now growing and grinding grain alone does not mean we can presume the existence of bread; however, a group of burned stones nearby suggests that the grains were actually baked (rather than fermented or cooked to make a porridge-like dish).

This is exciting for two reasons. Firstly, up until the discovery, it had been widely assumed that the invention of bread coincided with the Neolithic Revolution (which was some 12,000 years later), when humans decided en masse it was more efficient to stay put and farm, as opposed to following a nomadic lifestyle. However, the Fertile Crescent archaeological findings suggest that humans were living in more permanent settlements much earlier than previously thought, but that it then took longer for stable agricultural practices to become the norm – hardly surprising when your tools are made from stone, and your tools to make those tools are also made from stone, which are also made from... probably best we stop there.

The second reason relates to the kind of grains that were found. People had been eating grasses and some wild forms of grain before this time, but it is not clear how these would have been consumed. Whereas, with einkorn wheat, we know it must have been cultivated, and we also know it is one of the only ancient grains that can be used to make leavened bread (for example, it is near-impossible to make leavened bread from barley alone, due to its low gluten content). But as to whether leavened bread existed this early on, we can only speculate. We do know that fermentation was practised, and there is now evidence to suggest that baked food existed, so we can only hope those early farmers knew what was good for them and baked delicious, leavened bread. To us, 22,500 years of bread-making history sounded about right.

Fast forward to 4000 BCE and bread-making was an everyday occurrence in what is generally considered to be the first city: Uruk, in Babylonia (now southern Iraq). Other regions throughout the Fertile Crescent, North Africa, Europe and Asia soon followed, adopting leavened bread as a reliable source of food to fuel their growing populations. Interestingly, the Egyptian and Indo-Aryan words for barley are relatively similar – *djot* and *djavas*, respectively – despite there being no trade routes linking the two cultures. Meanwhile, in South America, although early civilisations had also developed agricultural systems around 4000 BCE, the preferred crops were corn, quinoa, sweet potatoes and beans, which did not lend themselves easily to flour and bread-making.

Looking still further ahead, it's clear that bread was also a staple during the Greek and Roman eras. The first collection of recipes resembling a cookbook, *Apicius (or Apici Caeli De Re Coquinaria)*, was compiled in the first century, and includes many mentions of bread made from wheat. Fashion dictated that white bread was a sign of sophistication, and was reserved for the best households, whereas wholegrains, pulses, peas, fava beans, acorns and chestnuts were eaten by the poor. The Greek physician, Galen, recommended that white bread be the first choice, but that wholegrain bread might be eaten to pass a stool. Even in Homer's Odyssey, bread is used to distinguish between humans and gods. After Odysseus has thrown a discus very, very far, he turns to the crowds and says: 'I far excel every one else in the whole world, of those who still eat bread upon the face of the earth.' So, as well as being a tasty, daily essential, it appears that the very consumption of bread was fundamental to being human.

Even though further research turfed up studies that cite evidence of wild grain grinding over 100,000 years ago, we're satisfied knowing, with very near certainty, that humans were baking and enjoying bread at least 25,000 years ago – a wonderfully humbling thought to contemplate.

Thousands of years old, these images of Egyptian bakers kneading dough, filling moulds and harvesting grain, as well as Romans selling bread, seem very familiar

Gramineae (Hordeae.)

Triticum vulgare L.

W.Müller n.d.Nat.

The first grains grown to make bread
were barley, einkorn and emmer

Origins of butter

Butter is an altogether trickier topic, since it has been the subject of much less research and study. There are plenty of creamery instruction manuals, histories of dairy sculptures and food technology texts on margarine (but let us not linger on that unappealing product). It is, however, surprisingly difficult to find authoritative texts relating to the origins of butter.

As with bread, we can start with archaeology. We know the cultivation of plants occurred before the domestication of animals. Pre-historic civilisations (from around 12,000 BCE) went through transitional periods of nurturing farmland for crops, but still supplementing their diets through hunting. At the same time, other groups began to domesticate livestock while moving from place to place. These multiple modes of living continue today, with some nomadic herding peoples living not dissimilar lives to those of their early ancestors.

Some of the first animals to be domesticated, around 9000 BCE (11,000 years ago), were goats and sheep, probably because of their manageable size. This means that pre-historic butter must have been quite different to the yellow pats we're used to nowadays. Sheep's and goat's milk contain less carotene than cow's milk, so the butter made from them would likely have been much paler, with a sharper taste.

Sheep and goats were not the only source of butter, with records of milk from camels, yaks and reindeers also being used – both before and after cows were domesticated.

The change from hunting animals to domesticating them brought about many changes in how humans chose to live. Searing freshly hunted meat over an open fire was an early method of preservation (although not a terribly effective one, and needless to say, one which only applied when the hunt was successful). Searing was later surpassed by baking (or roasting), but trapping heat in an enclosed space involved collecting and assembling heat-conducting materials, which were often heavy and not particularly convenient for a nomadic lifestyle. This in part persuaded nomads to become more stationary, and although the animals could continue to be used as a resource for meat, as well as sacks from the skin, and bones made into fish hooks, combs and even flutes, the more prized animal product was milk. For this, animals needed to be reared and looked after.

Despite knowing all of this, there is no one time and place recognised by academics as the birthplace of butter. Instead, we have a variety of stories involving different animals and places. Amazingly enough, the technique for making butter appears to have been universal. Long before the invention of the milking pail, animal-skin pouches were used to store liquids. When herds and communities moved to new pastures, pouches containing milk would be slung over the backs of pack animals. In keeping with the loping motion of the animal, these pouches were swung from side to side, thus separating the creamy milk from the butterfat.

Numerous mythological texts refer to butter, such as the Hindu Samuthra Manthan, aka. 'The Churning of the Milky Ocean', and fantastic tales of yak butter being made accidentally by children kicking yak-skin sacks filled with yak milk.

Butter-making around the world at the same time (circa 1800) may look different, but the technique was universal

In Hindu mythology, the importance of milk, and more importantly, butter is alluded to in three scriptures: the Bhagavata Purana, the Mahabharata and the Vishnu Purana. These texts are written pieces of literature (as opposed to oral stories that have been passed down and later recorded in text form) and serve a purpose similar to that of a parable or fable.

Mythology aside, what we do know is that butter churning was commonplace well before the start of the Christian common era (CE) (more than 2000 years ago), but not necessarily with a culinary purpose. In Greek and Roman culture, butter was not relished or held in such acclaim as it was in Asia and northern Europe. In Apicius, *butyrum* (the Latin root of the word butter) is merely listed in the index, with no further explanation – and is only understood to be a reference to butter from the mentions of butyrum in physicians' handbooks of the time, which suggest using butter on burns and bruises or on dry skin as a moisturiser, although olive oil would still have been used for these purposes.

While butter was also used as a lubricant for axle grinding and as fuel for household lamps (which sounds both resourceful and sacrilegious), those who preferred to eat butter rather than golden olive oil were viewed as less refined. The Greek poet Anaxandrides derisively referred to barbarians from the north as 'butter-eaters' and 'milk-drinkers' – although it's important to note that eating cheese was, apparently, fine. It's thought that this discrepancy comes down to perishability: because it would have been difficult to store milk and butter, the assumption was that if you ate those foods you weren't too fussy about whether they were fit for consumption. Whereas not only was cheese safe to eat after being kept in grottos or caves (as is still customary

today), it actually improved during storage. As a result, having a penchant for cellar-ripened dairy delights became a way of demonstrating that you possessed important cultural capital. In northern Europe, attitudes to butter were less difficult to navigate: it was an esteemed, high-energy food, especially in Scandinavia, where it was often buried in bogs, both to preserve it and hide it from butter-hungry thieves. Butter has also been found alongside bodies buried in bogs, which are thought to have been sacrifices to the gods, but it is unclear whether the butter was in some way connected with the death, potentially intended as an offering, or was entirely unrelated. Perhaps drawing his inspiration from these age-old butter-burying practices, Samuel Pepys is known to have hidden a wheel of Parmesan in his garden during the Great Fire of London.

Whether eaten or slathered on the skin, butter soon spread across many early civilisations throughout Europe and Asia.

By the early Middle Ages, as communities became increasingly dependent on cattle farming for their income, we start to see butter appearing more frequently, most notably in medieval France. Since bread had already long established itself in the daily lives of many people, it would seem only natural that bread and butter be eaten together. But not so fast – that's not necessarily how it happened.

Butirum.

ſo.natur. c.7.h. meli ex eo & lacte peccorino. Iuuamenti.
conuer ſupfluitates pulmonis granatis per frigiditate a ſiccitate.
nocumentium. abetat ſtomacu remoto nocumti. cu reb; ſapi
cis.

Women selling bread and butter
was worthy of record in this
fourteenth-century illustration

Bread & butter: a new marriage

So how did bread and butter find their true partner? One glorious proposition would have us believe that the same sixteenth-century astronomer who first postulated that the Earth travels around the Sun also first paired bread and butter.

Rumour has it that Copernicus, who had been working as an economic administrator, played a key role in directing the defence when a castle in Olsztyn, north-eastern Poland, came under siege from the Teutonic knights. To add to an already tricky situation, the castle was simultaneously subjected to a nasty bout of the plague, putting Copernicus's plans at risk, as his soldiers were dropping like flies. Luckily for all concerned, Copernicus had earlier trained in medicine and he began to notice that only the soldiers who ate bread contracted the plague. Realising that the bread had to be carried up several flights of steps from the kitchen, and was often dropped on the way, Copernicus's inspired solution was to coat the loaves in a thin layer of churned cream. This meant it was possible to see which loaves had been dropped, and they could then be wiped clean (Copernicus was spookily ahead of his time here, since bacteria wasn't discovered for another hundred years...). Lo and behold, the plague was curbed, and a teatime treat invented in the process. Unfortunately, this apocryphal story has now been largely discredited, and we can but hope that Copernicus is content to be known for his astronomy-related achievements.

So, if Copernicus was not in fact the instigator of spreading butter on bread, where does that leave us? It is highly likely that buttered bread was eaten some time before it was recorded in writing for posterity; however, written records are the surest evidence we have. And with the popularisation of the printing press in the first half of the fifteenth century, the number of cooking and household management texts grew exponentially, with the genre firmly established by the early eighteenth century.

Intriguingly, though, one of the earliest mentions of bread and butter happens to be in the first treatise written about fly fishing. Now, anyone who has ever gone fishing knows the importance of having appropriate sustenance with them – and such was the advice of Juliana Berners, writing 'The Treatyse of Fysshynge wyth an Angle' towards the end of the fifteenth century, and printed in *The Boke of Saint Albans*:

Browne breede tostyd wyth hony in lyknesse of a butteryd loof.

Thrilled as we were to learn that the first mention of bread and butter eaten together was in a passage about fishing written by a dame, delving a little deeper revealed there was more to this than met the eye. It is widely suspected that the treatise in question was the work of multiple authors, especially as it only appeared in the second (1496) edition of the book, published by Wynkyn de Worde, who worked alongside William Caxton and may well have exercised considerable artistic license.

For our next account (albeit concerning buttered toast, rather than bread, but let's not split hairs here), we have Fynes Moryson, writing in 1617, and later quoted by Elizabeth David, among others: 'All within the sound of Bow Bell, are in reproch called cochnies, and eaters of buttered tostes.'

It is truly incredible to look up at the looming skyscrapers of London's business district and imagine buttery-fingered villagers crunching on toast before the area even had so much as a port. And still more delightful to learn that that the consumption of bread and butter to counter the excesses of members of parliament appears to be a long-standing tradition, perhaps superseded today by the ubiquitous kebab! Note Samuel Pepys, who writes in his diary entry for 5th June 1661, of a post-work game of bowls and the susequent 'drinking of great draughts of claret, and eating botargo and bread and butter till 12 at night, it being moonshine; and so to bed, very near fuddled.'

After reading hundreds of recipes and accounts of bread- and butter-making, what continues to astound us is how much remains the same. The difference now being the ancient techniques are used out of choice rather than necessity. Bread had to be left to prove so it would create a light loaf, cream had to be left to separate (and ferment in the meantime). Today, we have the technology to speed up these processes, but conversely we're returning to the old methods with a sense of wonder and delight. We're seeing the benefits of the traditional methods and understanding that it is not always best to cut corners when you're aiming to achieve maximum flavour and pleasure.

A panel from Arthur Szyk's 1927 'Statute of Kalisz' series of paintings entitled *Jewish Craftsmen and Tradesmen* (right) depicts a baker in 1264, but could just as easily show any of The Snapery Bakery's bakers. The various products are neatly shaped and lined up on a peel (the wooden board used to transfer loaves), ready to be slid into the oven. The baker looks strong and hard-working, with a furrowed brow and a look of concentration on his face – and the proof of his labours stacked behind him: row upon row of domed loaves sitting prettily on the shelves, no doubt ready to be buttered.

Production & craft

Here we burrow deeper into bread and butter's rich and diverse story, taking a whistle-stop tour through changing making methods and dining cultures, starting in the sixteenth century and travelling right through to the present day.

Early recipes

From around 1500 to today, there have been huge shifts for bread and butter in terms of the range of recipes, cultural importance and, of course, commercial manufacturing. For every point of difference, however, there seems to be a similarity. The economic growth spurts of the sixteenth century, for example, were apparently accompanied by the same extremes of excess and scarcity that we see today (although, perhaps there are fewer butter sculptures these days).

Roman chef Bartolomeo Scappi writes about a 1536 feast that saw the creation of butter sculptures of 'an elephant with a palanquin, Hercules with a lion and a Moor seated on a camel', while at the same time peasants were eating coarse bread made from bran and chaff, and sometimes even hay and straw.

From a general food history perspective, the sixteenth century is a very exciting time, as this is when we start to see recipes being written down, developed and adapted – in short, food writing begins to take root and grow. These texts give us a unique insight into what was culturally important at the time. For example, what was the equivalent of a haute cuisine tuile? Or, contrastingly, what might be considered an early modern chicken nugget?

At this time, butter was still used for medicinal purposes, as explained by Andrew Boorde, a contemporary physician: 'Butter made of cream is moist of operation, it is good for the chest and lungs and also it does relax and mollify the belly, Dutch men eat it all the time.' But, despite its bodily uses, it was also becoming more commonly and creatively used in the kitchen. Gilly Lehman, in her essay on culinary history as an exciting new field, notes the boom in baking during this period, with more than 50 per cent of recipes written after 1545 containing butter.

By the eighteenth century, bread and butter had become a permanent fixture in well-to-do households across Europe, and baking was firmly embedded in everyday culture, with scones, shortbread and Chelsea buns all being invented during this time. Additionally, the increase in affluence from trading meant that teatime treats were not just available to the wealthy but also to an emergent middle class, giving professional bakers and butter-makers a new creative freedom. Bakers began to experiment with fruited brioches, saffron buns and gingerbread, taking advantage of the newly available exotic ingredients, such as treacle and currants.

Another factor contributing to the baking boom, catalysed by a rise in the middle class, was the increasing interest in home baking. In Sara Pennell's fascinating book, *The Birth of the English Kitchen, 1600–1850*, she explains how domestic ovens were the most common addition to ranges and hearths towards the end of the eighteenth century. Prior to this, it was common to make dough and then take it to a baker's oven for baking, but having a kitchen oven offered much more opportunity for experimentation. Many classic dishes we're still fond of have become locked into our collective consciousness through countless iterations of recipes noted at this time. A great example is bread and butter pudding.

Bread and butter pudding was also known as 'whitepot', from the whiteness of the cream the pudding swims in before it is baked, and the recipe can be traced back to the thirteenth century.

However, all good seventeenth-century household-management guides contain at least one, and both Eliza Smith's *The Compleat Housewife* and Hannah Woolley's *A Queen Like Closet* both include multiple versions, so the reader can choose the right pudding for the occasion. This touches on another significant culinary shift during this time: the introduction of sugar, which undoubtedly gave the baking and dairy trades a boost.

To learn a little more about early modern recipes, I looked to Gervase Markham's *The Well-Kept Kitchen*. Mr Markham is known to have written extensively, if not entirely accurately, about husbandry and house-keeping in the seventeenth century. He also happens to have edited *The Boke of Saint Albans* – which, as you may recall, holds our first historical reference to bread and butter, written by one Juliana Berners. A very happy coincidence indeed.

What's clear from Markham's recipes is that the Roman and Greek tradition of white bread for the rich and brown bread for the poor still applied. In his recipe for manchet (a name for the best quality, small sweet breads that would be made out of white flour), there is a distinct emphasis on purity and cleanliness. As he writes [the emphasis is ours]: '...first your meal, being ground upon the black stones... which makes *the whitest* flour, and bolted through

the finest bolting cloth, you shall put it into a *clean* kimnel... put into it of *the best* ale barm...'

In contrast, his brown bread recipe begins, 'For your brown bread, or bread for your hind servants…', showing clearly the class divide, with those who were perceived to be more refined eating refined bread, while the more fibrous breads were reserved for those whose constitutions were deemed able to withstand the heartier grains.

Interestingly, suet is the fat of choice for Markham's desserts, and neither his bread pudding or gingerbread recipes use butter. However, there is a recipe for a sweet butter sauce entitled, 'To roast a pound of butter well'. The concept of roasting butter baffled me (surely, it must melt and drip everywhere?) and so I delved a little deeper, only to discover several more recipes, one of which, from Hannah Glasse's 1747 *The Art of Cookery Made Plain and Easy*, is given here: 'Lay it [the butter] in Salt and Water two or three Hours, then spit it, and rub it all over with Crumbs of Bread, with a little grated Nutmeg, lay it to the Fire, and as it roasts, bathe it with the Yolks of two Eggs, and then with Crumbs of Bread all the Time it is a roasting; but have ready a pint of Oysters stewed in their own Liquor, and lay in the Dish under the Butter when the Bread has soaked up all the Butter, brown the Outside, and lay it on your Oysters. Your Fire must be very slow'. This is a recipe I have yet to try…

As popular as bread and butter had become by this time, not everyone was convinced. Horse Bread (page 112), a heavy bread made from bran, rye and fava bean flour, was still widely considered to be only suitable for horses, pigs and other livestock. This meant that a growing number of people went hungry, rather than eat bread with a lowly status, despite its nutritional value. Observing this in 1771, an unnamed critic from Salisbury wrote a very strongly worded essay on the pitfalls of 'modern luxury', claiming that bread, butter and tea were largely to blame for societal demise. Our unhappy author writes: 'Not content with fine bread, the poor country cottager pampers her appetite by covering it with *butter*; and her thrift must be solaced with the juice of the leaves of that Indian shrub (which I most heartily wish had never found an entrance into these kingdoms) commonly called Tea. Hysterics, a disorder unknown to the former ages, but now the Idol of the Medical Fraternity, take their force source from this noxious herb…'.

And he goes on to deride the quality of flour received from mills: 'We are now compelled to eat what is called white bread, composed partly of fine flour, with other ingredients concealed within the mystery of the baker, as witness, the lime, the chalk, the allum, with others perhaps less wholesome, which often make their way through the vehicle called the Mill… the fine hotch-potch of the mill destroys more of its inhabitants than all the swords and fire-arms now wielded in America'.

Bold claims. And yet the writer is perhaps entitled to feel somewhat hard done by. As the popularity of baked goods grew, the demand for bread outstripped the still relatively rudimentary wheat-farming methods, meaning that flour supplies were low. As such, bakers saw fit to adulterate their flour with the likes of chalk, allum, plaster of paris, pea flour and potato flour – all much cheaper than wheat flour. Moreover, bakers were known for short-changing their customers and often providing inedible produce, so unfortunately I cannot show solidarity by leaping to their defence. But a favourite claim of our passionate friend has to be the following observation on the

fertility of the local population, no doubt linked to bread and butter consumption: 'The poor people do not now carry on life as they did formerly. They were then honest, industrious, sober, frugal and careful… they were contented to live at the smallest expense and instead of Tea and Bread and Butter and the finest flour, the woman of the house seldom knew any greater repast than bread made of an equal mixture of Bran and flour, and happy, very happy to arrive at this! Butter was then a stranger to the poor man's house… How common in those days, for the man and his wife to breed a family of five or six children… how usual in the present, to apply to the overseers even tho' there are but two!… Let good, wholesome, plain, coarse bread, with a due mixture of bran and flour, again be introduced and if the poor man will not be at the pains of making it at his own house, permit not the baker, on any pretence whatsoever, under a very heavy penalty, to sell any better (pardon me) I mean *finer* bread'.

Oh dear, he really didn't like bread and butter at all.

Changing fashions

Despite the lack of enthusiasm of a minority, by the end of the eighteenth century, bread and butter had become a popular snack popped on a toasting fork and slathered with butter. The adjective bread-and-butter, to describe steady, financially dependable work, also came into use during this period.

By the turn of the century, new developments in the commercial production of bread and butter were taking place, developments that created a multitudinous variety.

Up until this point, bakehouses and brew-houses were found next door to each other, and the yeast used in both beer and bread were one and the same. With increased demand came the impetus for a wider variety of products, and bakers discovered that differing strains of yeast created different textures and flavours of bread, much the same as with beer. Where previously bakers and brewers had been joined at the hip, bakers gained a measure of independence, and their experimentation with different starter cultures and yeasts often proved fruitful, and profitable. Not only this, but the invention of baking powder in the first half of the nineteenth century saw an increase in cake and bread consumption, with Victoria sponge, Battenberg and Welsh cakes all dating from this time.

Along with this increase in variety came strong opinions on which ones should or should not be eaten fueling the pressure of fashion (and keeping up with it). We see in the scene (right), from Act II, Scene II of Oscar Wilde's *The Importance of Being Earnest* what a societal blunder being served the 'incorrect' teatime morsel would have been:

Cecily: ...May I offer you some tea, Miss Fairfax?

Gwendolen: (with elaborate politeness) Thank you. (Aside) Detestable girl! But I require tea!

Cecily: (sweetly) Sugar?

Gwendolen: (superciliously) No, thank you. Sugar is not fashionable any more [Cecily looks angrily at her, takes up the tongs and puts four lumps of sugar into the cup]

Cecily: (severely) Cake or bread and butter?

Gwendolen: (in a bored manner) Bread and butter, please. Cake is rarely seen at the best houses nowadays.

Cecily: [cuts a very large slice of cake and puts it on the tray] Hand that to Miss Fairfax.

[Merriman (the butler) does so... Gwendolen drinks the tea and makes a grimace. Puts down cup at once, reaches out her hand to the bread and butter, looks at it and finds it is cake. Rises in indignation]

Gwendolen: You have filled my tea with lumps of sugar, and though I asked most distinctly for bread and butter, you have given me cake. I am known for the gentleness of my disposition, and the extraordinary sweetness of my nature, but I warn you, Miss Cardew, you may go too far.

Of course, Wilde is highlighting the absurdity of such attachment to a food choice. That what one eats could say so much about a person seems ludicrous. And yet Gwendolen's outrage is entirely relatable.

Using the Acmé stove, Colonel Wyvern assures the reader they can bake a good loaf of bread in less than half an hour

One outcome of this commercialisation was the plethora of products that were newly assigned cultural capital. The influx was marked, making it all the more important to display your awareness of what was in fashion, if you were to maintain a semblance of social standing.

Interestingly, the preference for white bread over brown still prevailed. In nineteenth century America, Dr Alvin Wood Chase writes, in his *Third, Last and Complete Receipt Book*: 'If bread is heavy – not light and porous – or if it is sour, it is only fit for the pigs... A loaf of perfect bread, white, light, sweet, tender, and elastic, with a golden brown crust, is a proof of high civilisation.' Dr Chase, an physician, makes no bones about polarising 'good' and 'bad' bread, and is also very quick to ensure that 'fragrant, highly-flavoured butter of May or June' be served by the mistress of the house. Given that refrigerators were not commercially available until 1913, it might have been a bit tricky to consistently provide the May butter Dr Chase recommends, but we're sure the lady of the house did the best she could.

This affinity with white bread can be seen wherever nations were subject to colonisation: South African *potbrood*, *petit pain* in Cambodia and Jamaican *hardo* bread. Those who were sent to colonise were often accustomed to eating bread and butter, and would go to great lengths to ensure they could maintain their creature comforts abroad. Colonel Wyvern, in his *Culinary Jottings for Madras* tells of his friend's assurances that 'good bread was the back-bone of happiness – gustatory happiness, that is to say – in the jungle', and he goes on to explain in some detail how an adventurer might make a good bread roll with American or Australian imported flours, Yeatman's baking powder, butter, milk and salt, baked in an Acmé stove. Colonial-outpost baking was perhaps not for everyone, but we can still its repercussions today. William Rubel, in his book *Bread: A Global History,* notes how manufactured brown breads are still relatively new in Asian markets, since the breads that were introduced by the colonisers were all made from white refined flour.

Industrial Revolution

We have yet to touch on perhaps the most dramatic shift for the commercial manufacture of bread and butter, which can be encapsulated in one word: scale. Although the Industrial Revolution started with the textile industry, the sheer increase in population worldwide meant that new methods of production were required to keep up with the demand for food.

Centrifugal milk separators, refrigeration, pasteurisation, combine harvesters, balers, steam trains and ships (to transport grain across the Atlantic), grain purifiers, roller mills, steam-powered flour mills, plansifters, commercial yeast, self-raising flour, margarine, the Boland kneader – all were products of the Industrial Revolution and all led to bread and butter being made in much greater quantities than ever before. Note that we're talking about increased quantity here, not necessarily quality. This was the first time the commercial potential of food could be realised on such a scale, and often this meant a de-prioritisation of flavour and craft, in return for scalability and profits.

For butter, the turning point came with the discovery that centrifugal forces could separate cream from milk. Before this, cows would be milked and the milk would be left to sit for a day or so. During this time, the cream would rise to the surface and be skimmed off in a process called 'hand-skimming' (which is coming back

Before mechanised milk churners, above, cream was left to separate and ferment naturally, giving butter a tangy, sometimes cheesy taste

into fashion today). At the same time, the cream would naturally begin to ferment, giving the butter a tangy, almost cheesy flavour – now sought after in artisan cultured butter.

It is unclear who first demonstrated the possibility of separating the cream from milk by spinning it around very, very quickly, but the discovery is often attributed to Swiss inventor Gustaf de Laval, who began to produce the machines commercially towards the end of the nineteenth century. When this happened, large-scale creameries started to pop up all over Europe, the US and Canada. This then meant that women could get more money from sending their milk to creameries than they could from selling their butter. It also meant that butter became milder in flavour, partly because the cream was not left to ferment before churning and partly because less salt was used. In traditionally made 'cultured' butter, the generous salting would go some way to preserving the more bacteria-rich butter, but with the fresher, unfermented cream used in commercially manufactured butter, the salt only needed to act as a flavour enhancer.

Advances in refrigeration and transportation meant that butters with distinctive local tastes could be enjoyed further afield. The Cork Butter Exchange facilitated the supply of local butter across Britain and Ireland, much to the delight of metropolitan elites. And when the 10,000 mills in the UK – as there were by 1900, compared to more like 20 today – were unable to meet the demand from bakers, steam ships could carry extra supplies of wheat across the Atlantic. The relaxation of Britain's Corn Laws (laws that determined the price of grain based on its origin, favouring local grain) in 1846 paved the way for this trade. What millers could not have predicted was the US wheat being much tougher than soft European wheat and

needing different milling equipment, hence the invention of different machines for grinding and winnowing the grain. Mills moved closer to port towns to take advantage of these new grain imports.

In essence, these industrialised techniques meant more consistent, transportable and therefore more reliable products. Products, as opposed to homely sustenance, which could be marketed and distributed wherever the infrastructure existed. Developments in home-cooking equipment, namely ovens, meant more comprehensive cooking in the home, but the domestic consumer shifts were broadly overshadowed by the scaling of mass-market goods at that time, which, for better or worse, has very much influenced how we continue to think of food today.

The wartime slice

As we continue our journey, it's important to explore how the World Wars affected bread and butter consumption and production, as both wars had a huge impact.

By the beginning of the twentieth century, technological advances meant that mass-produced bread and butter were found in most households. However, such abundance came to an end with the outbreak of war in 1914. Since it was anticipated that the conflict would not last long, neither side planned for the effect on food supplies. As the war took hold, the impact was felt on the battlefields as well as on the home front: both sides grossly underestimated the amount of food needed to feed their troops; and, with men fighting in the trenches, the number of agricultural workers was also greatly diminished, resulting in significantly reduced grain harvests.

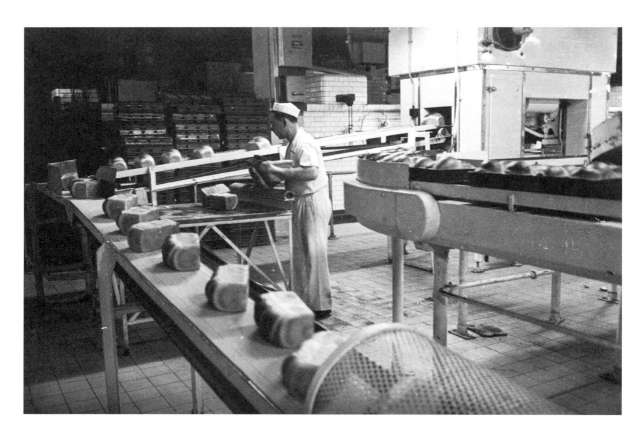

Using the Chorleywood process, a loaf of
sliced white bread can be made in just ninety
minutes. It can be packaged and ready for
distribution within three hours – much like this
line of baked loaves at the Wonderloaf Bakery,
London in 1965

In Britain, the Ministry of Food put in place measures to safeguard the supply of grains, importing wheat from the US and Canada to replace the embargoed Russian grain. Millers and bakers had to use wheat sparingly, and so wheat flour was often supplemented with oats, rye, barley, soya and potato flour, resulting in a darker and heavier loaf that came to be known as 'War Bread'. By now, bread and butter were seen as fundamental to the way we eat, and although the availability of bread was never restricted, butter was one of the first foods to be rationed. And it wasn't just ordinary people who were affected. Ration books were given to everyone, including King George V, who is thought to have inspired the rather lovely poem by A.A. Milne, *The King's Breakfast*.

Nobody,
My darling,
Could call me a fussy man –
BUT
I do like a little bit of butter
to my bread!
– A.A Milne

Even after the end of the hostilities, food remained in short supply, and a global recession meant that unemployment was widespread – 'on the breadline' (meaning to be close to poverty) came into use around this time. By the mid-1930s things were starting to look up, with the strictures on grain supply that led to the baking of War Bread easing. Around the same time, the invention of packaging machines for bread and butter saw a doubling of butter consumption between 1909 and 1936. The respite was short-lived, however.

As World War II tightened its grip in the UK, rationing resumed in January 1940, and butter was again rationed. National Butter was provided to households, as well as two sorts of National Margarine, and it was common to mix butter and margarine together, to give the margarine a buttery taste and to make the butter go further. My [Eve] grandmother grew up in an industrial part of the country and I vividly remember her telling me that there would always be two spreads on the table: if you were working (and bringing in money), you were allowed butter; if not, you were given margarine (more likely a mixture of margarine and animal fats). With white flour in short supply, the National Loaf, made from wholemeal flour, was introduced in 1942 and, despite its unpopularity, would remain in place until 1956.

Machine takeover

The end of rationing was, of course, welcomed by households, but it also paved the way for the resumption of industrial food manufacturing. As investment in food production led to new ways of making bread and butter, speed was deemed to be the most important factor, along with a need to bake with a lower protein flour. Digestibility, flavour and the use of natural preservatives all took a back seat.

During the war, British bakers had grown used to baking with flour milled from American and Canadian wheat, which had a higher protein content and so built gluten easily, producing well-structured loaves. This meant that the cheaper and more plentiful local wheat was less in demand. The baking industry's response was to devise a method of making bread that was quick and could use low-protein wheat. And so, in 1961, the Chorleywood process was born.

In one fell swoop, the manufacturing time of a loaf of sliced white bread went from a day to ninety minutes. Through a combination of adding vitamin C, fat and baker's yeast to the dough, and using high-speed mixers, the need for bulk fermentation was eliminated. The result was a white, pappy loaf with a soft mouthfeel. By the 1980s, the reach was global: from a Vietnamese banh mi to a Mexican bolillo, processed white bread had become ubiquitous. Today, the Chorleywood process is responsible for producing more than 80% of our bread.

For centuries before this, bakers had considered time as necessary an ingredient as flour, water or salt when it came to making bread, for three main reasons. Firstly, when the dough is left to prove, the proteins in the flour are broken down, making the bread easier to digest (this is why sourdough bread may be tolerated by those with gluten sensitivities – it's not gluten-free, of course, but it will likely be lower in gluten than most commercial bread).

Secondly, when food is given time, it develops in flavour. When dough sits at just above room temperature, enzymes break down the starch in the flour to make sugars, which the naturally occurring bacteria in the starter culture (most commonly lactobacilli) feed on, producing the lactic acid and acetic acid (vinegar) that gives sourdough bread its characteristic tangy taste. In a beautifully symbiotic way, the wild yeasts in the starter culture feed on different sugars, meaning there are plenty to go around. As the yeasts in sourdough leaven will likely vary from bakery to bakery, so does the flavour, opening the door to experimentation with different strains of yeast – just as winemakers and brewers already do to great effect.

Thirdly, the lactic acid acts as a natural preservative. A sourdough loaf kept in an airtight container will keep well for at least three days, and will make good toast for a week.

Although bread produced using the Chorleywood method might not sit well with many bakers, some credit has to be given for the resulting reduction in the price of a standard loaf. The authors of *Bread: A Slice of History* point out that, in 1847, a loaf of bread might have cost Jane Eyre a third of her daily income.

For butter the story is slightly different, inventions such as the 'butyrator', a large scale churner that took its name from the Latin, *butyrum*, meaning butter, enabled butter producers to increase their butter output ten-fold since the 1940s. While the scale of production has increased, the actual method has not changed vastly since creameries became the main source of butter in the late nineteenth century.

Towards the end of the twentieth century, production plateaued and focus started to shift toward a different angle altogether. Consumers began to cotton on to the effects that mass-production has on flavour, despite the positive impact it had on their wallets, and slowly but surely, the next generation of bakers and butter-makers began experiments in the kitchens that would lead to something much, much better.

Over the few hundred years we've covered, it becomes clear that our daily bread and butter has taken many higgledy-piggledy twists and turns on its journey. The effort expended along the way, to provide us with loaves on shelves and pats in fridges, is quite humbling – and we are surrounded by reminders of this history in our towns and cities today. Perhaps you've walked down Bread Street or Bun Alley, maybe you've visited Battenberg or Genoa, and likely not given too much thought to the buttery, flour-based concoctions behind these names. And why would you, the cake is there to be eaten, not philosophised over, after all.

This man is piling mass-produced butter on to a conveyor at a Campbeltown dairy, in Scotland, in 1950

Bread & butter today

We don't think it's a stretch to say that interest in bread and butter has risen in an unprecedented way, and we'd like to share a few ideas on why that might be…

In Elizabeth David's *English Bread and Yeast Cookery*, the author wonders if there is ever a time where 'household bread baking is never in decline', and we rather wish we could meet Elizabeth now and show her the plethora of home-baking TV shows and local classes bursting with people learning how to bake and churn. And then walk her around the area where The Snapery Bakery is based in Bermondsey, London, to show her the five small-scale bakeries in a radius of just as many miles.

There are all manner of reasons for this renewed interest in traditional methods and the resulting loaves and pats, and we will touch on just a few.

Let's start with the rise in 'eating local' – something that's commonly seen as attractive based on the assumption that local is better. 'Better' meaning sustainably grown, fairer for farmers, low food miles, more nutritious, more socially virtuous… the list goes on. Whether this is entirely accurate is perhaps best tackled by another book. But there's no doubt that 'locavores' are fuelling demand in neighbourhood markets and shops in their bid to support local makers and make better food-buying choices.

It's also easy to note a shift in consumer attitude towards food that is healthy. We are more aware of what we're putting in our bodies than ever before, and sourdough bread and real butter has certainly had plenty of good press. Sourdough is easy to digest and low-gluten due to the long proving time, and butter will not, it turns out, give you a heart attack (unless you cook and eat every recipe in this book!).

Finally, the last 30 years has seen incredible, global advances in technology and innovations in food production that could hardly have been imagined just a century ago. Alongside this modernity, there's a counter drive to preserve and appreciate the lessons of the past. There is a lot to be said for the continuation of ancient production techniques, and as a society, we are learning to value and return to these methods.

However, despite these plentiful shifts in attitude, we think it's fair to say that people do not solely base their food choices on locality, impact on health or interest in preserving tradition. There is something else at play, something more base, more simple: flavour.

It is flavour that motivates producers out of bed early and keeps them up at night. And it is flavour that has the taste-hunters traipsing across continents, countries and cities in search of the next bite. On the advantages of embracing flavour, Brillat-Savarin writes, 'gourmandism is the common bond which unites the nations of the world… It is gourmandism which sends wines, spirits, sugar, spices, pickles, salted foods and provisions of every kind, down to eggs and melons, across the earth from pole to pole… it is gourmandism which forms the livelihood of the industrious throng of cooks, confectioners, bakers and others…'.

For foods so simple, the enjoyment is exponential. One might expect to feel immense satisfaction from a decadent gâteau or rare breed steak, but in fact you might experience as much, if not more pleasure, from a crusty slice thick with spread.

Bread and butter in restaurants and homes has become immeasurably better. In recent years, metropolitan restaurants are providing more flavoursome bread and butter at the beginning of a meal. And rightly so. This is the first thing a diner eats and first impressions count. It has only been relatively recently that you might read a restaurant review where the critic leaves singing the praises of the bread and butter, be it a plain sourdough and classic butter, or a more ambitious slice alongside a butter showcasing a local ingredient or exotic flavour. Either way, if a small plate with something well-baked accompanied by a golden yellow round is put on the table shortly after you sit down, you know you will eat well.

But of course, it is not just restaurant meals that start with bread and butter. People all over the world start their days with hot, buttery toast. It is quick, cost-efficient and tasty – the triumvirate of modern cooking. But we wholeheartedly believe the crux of it is the flavour that keeps bread and butter in daily favour. Baguettes are nearly as popular in Tokyo as in Paris, cultured butter is just as prized in Normandy as in Stockholm, and sourdough sales are soaring from San Francisco to San Sebastian.

Good bread is the most fundamentally satisfying of all foods; and good bread with fresh butter, the greatest of feasts. – James Beard

If we have not bought our bread and butter, we have most certainly made it. The immense, almost greatest joy comes in the making. On making, we are only just scratching the surface. Pots and vats and tubs of fizzy flours and live creams can lead to such exciting and novel flavours – the kind that light up a sweet spot in your brain when you get it right.

There are endless combinations of bacteria when mixed with different ingredients and temperatures that will create breads and butters unlike that which you could ever buy.

For kitchen explorers, the pleasure of making bread and butter today is also increasingly in the physical. It's undeniably fun and entertaining to try a new technique, slapping dough onto the kitchen table or hand squeezing buttermilk out of fresh butter. It is as if we are only just realising that the bafflement, intrigue and delight we derive from the physical act of baking is just as much part of the fun as the pleasure of eating.

In bread and butter, there is something which reminds us of the simple joy of real food – at its root, it does not have to be so complicated. Whether out or at home, whether bought or made, from small-scale producers or home cooks, bread and butter is all about flavour, in an ambrosial, satisfying slice.

Global tastes & traditions

Multiculturalism is an inextricable and welcome part of modern life, and there's no better lens through which to explore diversity than food.

Bakers and butter-makers all over the globe are known for their obsessive and dedicated approach to their wares. Many are perfectionists, and often what starts out as a hobby takes hold, persuading the amateur to sacrifice many hours of sleep and socialising time in order to become a professional.

Richard and Grant spend days refining and tweaking their products and it only takes a short walk around any farmers' market to see that the same is true of most producers, no matter where you are. Whether making Scotch eggs in England, *khinkali* in Georgia, or *pão de queijo* in Brazil, all these producers come across as equally dedicated and obsessed.

Seeing this led us to explore the manifestations of bread and butter in different countries and cultures. Of course, we found the variety to be more plentiful in countries that have a longer history of dairy farming and grain milling, but it seems safe to say that nearly every culture relies on some kind of energy-dense bread-like product for sustenance, combined with a local fat – be it straight-up butter or butter combined with tallow, lard or vegetable fat.

Bread and butter translates wherever you are. In Mexico, *mantecado* is a slice of generously buttered white wheat bread dipped butter-side-down into white sugar. In Netherlands, *hagelslag* is a similar tradition except eaten at breakfast and the sugar is swapped for chocolate sprinkles. In Australia, fairy bread is sliced white buttered bread with multicoloured sprinkles on top of it. Understandably, these traditions have evolved independently – it's easy to see how one seeks to make a satisfying snack (bread and butter) into an indulgent one (bread, butter and sugar).

And at the same time as being in a world where we have so much in common across nations, there is still much localisation when it comes to bread and butter. Writing from the UK, it's easy to get caught up in thinking of bread as leavened, white wheat bread, and butter as cultured cow butter. And this is certainly true for most European or North American readers. It is also true for those reading in South America, Africa or the Asia Pacific region where mass-produced white bread is the norm, a repercussion of previous colonising activities.

It feels important to call out that, in this book at least, we still consider bread to be bread whether leavened or unleavened, as is more common in the Near East, Central Asia, the Arabian Peninsula, in some Mediterranean locales and the Indian subcontinent. And butter is still butter, made from any kind of animal milk and whether it is cultured, clarified or buried in a bog.

Some definitions in other food writing recently tries to narrow the definitions for foodstuffs to very specific regions or cultures, in the name of preservation, but in the case of bread and butter, and this is a large part of the appeal, there is no way to pin it down and say here is *the* bread and butter.

We hope this survey of breads and butters from around the globe will both stimulate your curiosity and whet your appetite. When it comes to 'mind over matter', if the matter in question is a hot, crunchy piece of toast drenched in butter, then matter will always win, in our experience.

Eurasia & Australasia

Bread

Baguette The classic French bread: a long, thin, typically white loaf with a golden crust. The flûte is a thicker version, and the ficelle a thinner version. Stories of its origin vary from Napoleon's men needing more transportable bread that they could fit in their uniform pockets, to metro-workers needing tearable bread after violent outbursts caused knives to be banned from the Paris metro. Either way, in 1920 a law was passed stipulating that bakers were not allowed to begin work before 4am, which meant they needed to devise a shape of bread that could be ready in time for when the bakery opened, and so the baguette became the standard loaf. Today, French law dictates that a baguette should contain only flour, water, yeast and salt, and that for a shop to be called a boulangerie its baguettes must be mixed and baked on site. How reassuring.

Brioche Typically baked in small rolls or loaves, brioche is a white bread enriched with butter and eggs. Although it does probably trace its origins to northern France, brioche was once widely assumed to have come from the Brie region – but there is little-to-no evidence for this, and it is now thought that the old French verb *brier* (meaning to work or knead with a small, wooden tool called a brie) is the more likely etymological root of the word. Perhaps the most well-known historical reference to brioche is the oft-quoted 'Let them eat cake' (*qu'ils mangent de la brioche*) which, in Jean-Jacques Rousseau's posthumously published *Confessions*, is attributed to Marie-Antoinette.

However, the wife of Louis XVI would have been only nine years old at the time of writing, and it is now believed that the infamous words were actually uttered by Maria Theresa, wife of Louis XIV. Since the terms brioche and *pain bénit* ('blessed bread') were used interchangeably in France at the time, it is possible that it was a perfectly reasonable suggestion for the peasants to eat 'brioche'. Nonetheless, the unpopularity of the monarchy, and its subsequent demise, led to this notion of royal bread-snobbery becoming firmly cemented in the French popular consciousness.

Borodinsky A Russian dark rye sourdough loaf most commonly flavoured with coriander or caraway seeds, and occasionally fennel seeds. It is thought to have originated in the early twentieth century, with the earliest written recipes dating back to 1933.

Ciabatta An airy Italian bread, usually made with olive oil and is known for its holes – the product of a very hydrated dough, which is not given a long (if any) bulk-rise, and so the dough yeast is still active when the bread is baked.

Focaccia A yeasted flatbread made from high-gluten flour and olive oil, and commonly flavoured with rosemary and salt, or sometimes with olives, sage or star anise. Thought to have been one of the first leavened breads from the Mediterranean, it derives its name from the Roman *panis focacius*, which can be loosely translated as 'hearth bread' – in those days, the bread would have been cooked in the embers of the fire in the centre of the house.

Knäckebröd This Scandinavian rye crispbread was among the first crispbreads to be widely eaten when it became straightforward to manufacture, package and distribute them on an industrial scale.

Cottage loaf Virginia Woolf and George Orwell were both fans of this old-fashioned British bread, which is comprised of a small circular white loaf sitting happily atop a larger circular white loaf. In Orwell's essay 'In Defence of English Cooking', he writes: 'if there is anything quite as good as the soft part of the crust from an English cottage loaf… I do not know of it'.

Crumpets In one text on the history of bread, which shall remain nameless, it is stated that 'crumpets are of decreasing importance' but we hasten to disagree. Crumpets are a delicious cross between a bread and a pancake. They are cooked on a hot plate or griddle on one side only, until they are cooked through and developed their distinctive holes, which are particularly good for soaking up butter.

Dampfnudel This German steamed white bread can be eaten as a dessert or an accompaniment to a main course. Its place in history is marked by the Dampfnudeltor gate in Freckenfeld, Germany, which was erected after local baker Johannes Muck, and his wife and apprentice, made 1,286 dampfnudel to appease Swedish soldiers during the Thirty Years War. Thanks to these little buns, the town was spared further pillage and the legacy of the dampfnudel lives on.

English muffins Much enjoyed by Victorians, these small round griddled breads are split in half and toasted before being eaten – often with butter and jam, or topped with poached eggs and hollandaise sauce.

Farls A type of soda bread made with baking soda, buttermilk and often potatoes. A large circle of the dough is cooked on a hot plate, and then each person is served a quarter – hence the name, from the old Scots word, *fardell*, meaning a quarter.

Fougasse This French flatbread has slashes cut through the dough, giving it the appearance of a large leaf. Often flavoured, this bread is a cousin of the Italian focaccia.

Kanelbullar These European cinnamon buns are made from an enriched dough and are flavoured with cinnamon and often cardamom as well. The original kanelbullar likely came from Sweden, although other regional variations include Denmark's cinnamon snails, called kanelsnegle, and the Finnish korvapuusti, which confusingly translates to 'slap in the face'.

Pain de campagne This naturally leavened sourdough bread can be made from wheat flour or flours milled from ancient grains, typically with the addition of some bran or rye to give more texture or nuttiness. It is usually shaped into a round *boule* and is sometimes called *miche*, simply meaning 'loaf' in French.

Khubz/pitta A white or wholemeal flatbread made with yeast and baked in a very hot oven, so it puffs up to create a pocket, making space for delicious fillings such as falafel. The Arabic word for bread is *khubz*, which most commonly refers to pita or similar pitta-eqsue flatbreads.

Pretzels Said to have originated in a monastery in Italy in 610 BCE, the shape of the pretzel was supposedly intended to mimic the folded arms of a child in the position adopted for prayer at that time. Made by twisting long pieces of yeasted dough into this distinctive shape,

Woman Cutting Bread, 1879
by Christian Krohg

pretzels can be soft – as in the traditional German brezel, or *laugenbrezel,* which is boiled in lye to give it a darker, more appealing colour – or crisp, with a much lower hydration level, as in the smaller versions eaten as a snack, most commonly in the USA.

Oliebollen A traditional Dutch or Belgian doughnut, *oliebollen* literally translates as 'oil balls', and these crispy treats are now eaten in some form across Italy, Croatia, Slovenia and Serbia, most commonly at New Year's Eve. They are sometimes filled with raisins, apples or candied fruit – and when cooked with animal fat instead of oil are called *smoutebol*.

Pumpernickel A slow-baked coarse-grained rye loaf that hails from Westphalia in Germany. The word loosely translates to 'flatulence devil', a reference to the fibre-heavy nature of the bread. Traditionally baked at a low temperature for more than 24 hours, this allows plenty of time for the Maillard reaction (which occurs when amino acids and sugars are exposed to temperatures above 140°C/275°F and causes food to brown, making it look and taste delicious), creating a deeply flavoured loaf.

Hokkaido milk bread A very light, pillowy, enriched bread originating from northern Japan but eaten all over East Asia. The bread uses the Tangzhong method of making bread, which involves creating a roux from flour and water (or milk) and adding that to the active yeast at 65°C/149°F. This locks in moisture, so the bread stays softer for longer.

Roti or chapati The most common unleavened Indian flatbread, made from wholemeal flour and cooked on a hot plate called a *tava*. It is often left unsalted, to counter the spiciness of the curries it generally accompanies.

Rugbrød **Very popular in Denmark, this 100% rye sourdough bread often contains cracked rye kernels, linseeds, sunflower seeds and malted barley syrup, which gives it a distinctive dark colour and a nutty sweetness.**

Naan bread A leavened Indian flatbread cooked by slapping the stretched-out dough onto the inside of a hot tandoor oven. Tandoor ovens can typically reach around 900°C/482°F, so naan is very quick to cook, puffs up nicely and has a satisfyingly smoky flavour from the charcoals of the tandoor.

Challah A lightly enriched Jewish bread, which is plaited and often decorated with sesame or poppy seeds. Traditionally eaten at the beginning of the Sabbath, challah is most commonly available in bakeries on a Friday. The dough is enriched with eggs (rather than milk or butter), since Jewish dietary laws prohibit the consumption of dairy and meat products in the same meal. The shape of the dough is said to come from the days when households would each donate a small ball of dough to the priest and he would make the synagogue's bread by putting together the balls of dough to create a larger patchwork bread.

Nohut ekmeği This Turkish/Albanian bread is made using chickpea flour and a leaven from the naturally occurring yeast on the chickpeas. It is a dense loaf with a pleasant nutty flavour.

Mantou Similar to the filled *bao* and *baozi*, *mantou* are Chinese steamed buns made from white wheat flour. There are two popular stories about how they got their name: the first has it that their name is a cognate of the Persian *manty* (a small filled dumpling), suggesting that *mantou* probably travelled from the Middle East to China around the third century. The more exciting tale tells of a chancellor named Zhuge Liang who, retreating from a battle in the Three Kingdoms (close to modern-day Myanmar), needed to cross a dangerously fast-flowing river. Faced with the prospect of making a sacrifice to appease the river god so his men could safely cross, rather than kill any of his already depleted army, he decided to make *mantou* ('barbarian's head'), and throw the head-shaped buns into the river instead.

Daktyla A leavened wheat and cornmeal bread decorated with sesame or nigella seeds, which is very popular in Greece, Turkey and Cyprus. *Daktyla* literally means 'fingers', a name derived from the several deep cuts made into the dough during proving, so that the bread splays out like fingers as it bakes.

Shirmal A golden saffron-flavoured wheat flatbread served throughout Iran, Pakistan and northern India. The bread is very similar to naan bread but is sweet, made with sugar, milk and a hint of cardamom.

Shoti puri The Georgian equivalent of a baguette, shoti puri is a light, vaguely boat-shaped bread. It is still mostly cooked by skilled local bakers in a *tonay*, which is similar to a tandoor oven, with the bread being slapped directly onto the inside of the oven.

Lavash An Armenian unleavened flatbread cooked on the inside of a tandoor oven. Although soft when kneaded and cooked, the bread is rolled out very thinly, so it can be dried to a crisp and then stored for many months. It is a common choice for Armenian Eucharist ceremonies.

Paratha A decadent Indian flatbread made by creating layers of very thin chapati or roti dough, which are then smothered with ghee and fried to create a laminated effect. Usually made with wheat flour, but in some parts of India, such as Rajasthan, mung bean flour is more commonly used.

Sangak A large, rectangular sourdough flatbread from Iran. The name comes from the Persian for 'little stone', as the bread is cooked by placing the sheets of dough on little stones or gravel on the floor of the oven, which causes attractive dimples to appear across the expansive bread.

Yufka Similar to lavash, yufka is a Turkish unleavened flatbread made from wheat flour. The dough is rested for a long time so it can be rolled out very thinly with an *oklava* (a long, thin rolling pin) and used in layers to make delicious stuffed pastries called *börek*.

Damper This simple Australian soda bread of wheat flour, salt and water was originally made by stockmen when they were travelling long distances without access to fresh rations. The dough is first placed over spread coals and then buried in them until the bread is cooked through. Making damper is still a popular campfire activity in Australia today.

Butter

Cultured butter A solid, usually yellow fat made from churning fermented animal milk or cream, most commonly from cows but also goats, sheep, yaks or camels. The ingredients of a cultured butter are no more than the starter culture (either commercially bought or naturally occurring in yogurts and soured creams), cream and often salt. Adding the culture is a relatively recent adaptation. Before pasteurisation and refrigeration were the norm, bacteria present in dairies would naturally ferment cream sitting on top of milk, which would then be skimmed off the top and turned into tangy butter.

Beurre d'Isigny AOP Butter made using cow's milk from Manche and Calvados in northern France. The mineral-rich soil of the area produces nutrient-dense vegetation for the cows to munch on, and their milk in turn produces buttercup-yellow butter with a faint taste of hazelnuts. A Parisian gourmand in the early nineteenth century declared that beurre d'Isigny has 'an unctuousness that can be detected in all the ragouts'.

'Drawn butter', clarified butter and ghee
There are minor distinctions between these three products, but they are all made using a similar process. Butter is gently heated so that it separates into three components: butterfat, water and milk solids. 'Drawn butter' is butter in its melted state, sometimes with the milk solids removed; 'clarified butter' is melted butter, always with the milk solids removed; and ghee is clarified butter that has been heated further so the water evaporates and the butter can be stored for long periods. It also has a nuttier flavour, and in Ayurveda, is said to have healing properties that are especially helpful for bad digestion, skin problems and poor memory.

In Egypt, *samna baladi* is made in the same way as ghee, except using buffalo cream, so the end result is white instead of golden yellow.

Yak butter Common in the Tibet mountains, where it's widely used for making butter tea (page 184). Unlike cows, yaks won't 'let down' their milk unless the calf is suckling, and so the first sips of milk are given to the calf before the *dri* (female yak) is milked, and then the calf is allowed to take its fill throughout the day. The mother and calf are only separated at night so there is enough milk for the morning, and the relationship between yak and owner can continue.

Whey butter Butter made from whey rather than cream. Whey butter was first invented by cheese-makers as a means to use up the large quantities of whey leftover from making cheese. Today, very few dairies produce whey butter as it is labour-intensive – the butterfat content of whey is much lower than that of cream and so larger quantities of whey are required to yield the same amount of butter. Some believe it is a lighter, healthier alternative to normal butter, whereas others maintain that the benefits are limited, since it has a lower smoke point than butter.

Mound of Butter, 1875–1885
by Antoine Vollon

Africa

Bread

Khobz eddar A leavened bread made with wheat or semolina that is eaten across North Africa (particularly in Algeria) – especially during Ramadan, after fasting. The name means 'home bread', as this bread is commonly made at home, as well as being available in the markets.

Aish baladi One of the first leavened breads ever made, this is still being eaten in Egypt today. It looks similar to wholemeal pitta but has a stronger taste due to its sourdough starter, which would originally have been used for both baking and brewing. The name literally means 'life bread'… it is said that a life without this bread is not a life at all.

Injera Sitting comfortably between a crumpet and a pancake, injera is an Ethiopian sourdough flatbread made from a small black grain called teff. Plate-sized, it usually has a vibrant and tangy flavour that complements the dips and stews served on top of it.

Potbrood This South African white leavened wheat bread originates from Dutch colonial times. It takes its name, meaning 'pot bread', from the Dutch oven it is baked in, which is usually placed open coals.

Kisra Not to be confused with the Algerian unleavened flatbread called *kesra*, this is a very thin sourdough flatbread from Sudan made from sorghum (also known as *durra* or 'great millet'). The fermented sorghum dough, *ajin*, is spread out on a hot pan to cook. When cooked through on one side, the bread is removed from the pan so it is golden and crispy on one side but still soft and absorbent on the other.

Puff puff A white wheat, sweet, yeasted bread that is deep-fried so it puffs up. This doughnut-like bread is very popular in Nigeria and goes by other names in neighbouring countries. In Ghana it is called *bofrot* or *togbei*, in Liberia it is called *kala* and in the Congo it is called *mikale*.

Green mealie A steamed cornbread most commonly eaten in South Africa and made from a maize that has a slight green tinge to it. The bread can either be eaten as a sort of porridge or baked into a firmer loaf, which is eaten warm and spread with butter.

Butter

Shea butter Of course, shea butter is not made from milk of animals but from the nuts of the shea tree. When unrefined and dried in the sun, its natural colour is a very buttery yellow and it gets paler the more it is refined. It is commonly used in lotions and salves to take advantage of its moisturising properties but it is also frequently used for cooking, in much the same way as coconut oil. It can be used to fry meat and fish or to fry onions for the base of a curry. The taste is strong, but it is very high in vitamin A and is believed to have healing qualities when consumed on a regular basis.

Smen Similar to ghee, smen is a clarified butter from Morocco. Oregano is often added for its antifungal properties, as smen may be kept for months or even years. Smen is also fermented to enhance its flavour further and a ripe smen is said to have a similar taste to a good blue cheese.

Camel butter Butter made from camel's milk is not easy to come by, even for Saharan nomads – although it was likely one of the first types of butter to be made, when sacks of milk clashed against the flanks of pack animals as people moved from place to place. More common these days is the transformation of camel milk into cheese, such as Camelbert.

Gibde An unwashed cow's butter from Chad. Soured milk called *raib* is shaken inside a gourd for 1–2 hours. The butter popcorn is then collected and transferred to another empty gourd (or calabash), where it is stored. Its mild milky flavour lends itself to being used for cooking children's food and other simple dishes.

Keshda mosakhana An Egytian buttery cream, keshda mosakhana is made by heating high-fat milk, then cooling it by scooping up ladlefuls of the warm milk and pouring it back into the remaining milk so that it froths and foams. The cooled milk is then left to settle so that the cream can be skimmed from the top and saved. The firm cream is then sliced and served on top of pastries and desserts.

Niter kibbeh and tesmi Flavoured ghee is popular in north-east Africa, and these two examples are from Ethiopia and Eritrea, respectively. Ingredients infused into the butter during clarification include garlic, ginger, turmeric, basil, thyme, oregano, koseret (a herb of the verbena family, also known as 'butter clarifying herb'), fenugreek, cumin, coriander, cinnamon, nutmeg and cardamom.

Americas

Bread

San Francisco sourdough This wheat sourdough bread, most commonly made in a round shape, is popular across America and particularly in San Francisco, California. During the Californian gold rush of the mid-nineteenth century, migrants from France brought with them sourdough bread-making techniques. The Californians have since made it their own by increasing the amount of mature starter culture – containing *Lactobacillus sanfranciscensis* bacteria – to give the bread its characteristically tangy taste and a more open crumb.

Bagel A hand-sized ring of white wheat leavened bread which is boiled before being baked. The resulting bread is often a little crusty on the outside and satisfyingly chewy on the inside. Bagels originate from Jewish communities in Krakow as far back as the early seventeenth century. They are commonly coated in a mixture or seeds and seasoning, which is known as an 'everything' bagel, (everything can be garlic or onion salt, pepper, poppy seeds, sesame seeds, caraway seeds and/or pumpkin seeds).

Marraqueta This crispy white wheat roll is popular across South America, with an apocryphal story attributing it to two French brothers named Maraquette who were baking in late-nineteenth-century Chile. The small rolls are baked with four close together in the oven so they merge into mini-loaves when baked. It is unclear, even to Chileans, whether one marraqueta is four rolls stuck together, a pair of them, or a single roll.

Cornbread As the name suggests, this is a bread made from coarsely ground corn. Although eaten across the USA, it is particularly associated with the Southern states. Leavened with bicarbonate of soda rather than yeast, it is often quite cake-like, especially with the butter and sugar that is customarily added.

Pão de queijo This little cheese bread made with cassava flour hails from Brazil, although similar breads can be found in Argentina (*chipita*), Bolivia (*cuñapé*), Ecuador (*pan de yuca*) and Colombia (*pandebono*). Its main ingredients are cassava flour and cheese, so it's not strictly a bread, but is too delicious to exclude from this list. The indigenous peoples of the Americas had been making simple breads from cassava root long before Portuguese colonisation, but the cheese is thought to be a later addition.

Pebete This is a long, white leavened wheat bread roll from Argentina. A cross between a hot-dog roll and a milk roll, it is a relatively sweet bread, usually filled with ham, cheese, tomato and mayonnaise. The word pebete is synonymous with something akin to 'kiddo', 'tike' or 'small fry', perhaps because this sandwich is usually clutched in the sticky hands of small children.

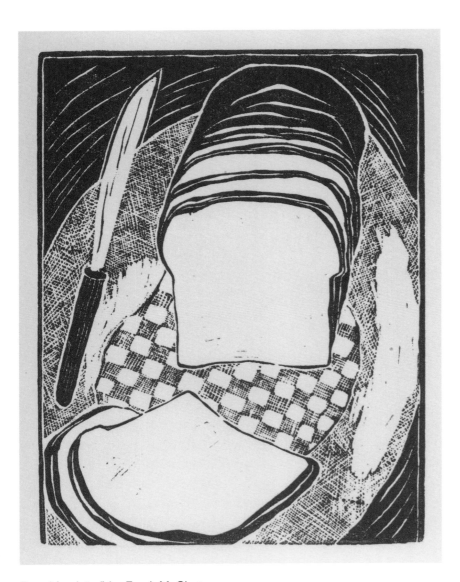

Bread (undated) by Frank McClure

Tortillas There are two types of this Mexican unleavened, disc-like bread: corn and wheat. As maize was cultivated in South America long before colonisation, the corn tortilla pre-dates the wheat tortilla; it can be made from white, yellow, blue or red corn, which needs to be soaked in a lime solution to nixtamalise (soften) it first. The alkaline nature of the lime makes the corn easier to grind into flour and enhances both its flavour and nutritional properties. The *masa harina* (maize flour) dough is then rolled out and cooked on a griddle. Wheat tortillas are made in much the same way, just using different flour and without the need for nixtamalising.

Hard dough or hardo bread
This a dense, sweet white wheat leavened bread from Jamaica. It is made in the same way as a normal white tin loaf but with added sugar. It is a staple in many Jamaican households and is eaten with savoury dishes such as ackee and saltfish or steamed callallo (a leafy green vegetable native to Jamaica), as well as sweet preserves such as guava jam.

Frybread Also known as 'elephant ears', this Native American bread is a leavened white wheat flatbread made from flour, salt, oil, water and baking powder or yeast. The dough is then deep-fried, filled and rolled up like a burrito. Commonly served at state fairs and festivals, it is famed for being highly calorific. Although now eaten at times of celebration, the bread was originally invented in the mid-nineteenth century, during the Navajo people's 300-mile walk, when the US government forcibly relocated them from Arizona to New Mexico. Along the way, with their usual diet of vegetables and beans unavailable, they were provided with limited rations, among which were the ingredients for frybread – a somewhat bittersweet story.

Butter

American butter Also known as sweet cream butter, American butter is made in much the same way as cultured butter, except that the cream is not fermented and so it lacks the tang or sourness of cultured butter. US law stipulates that butter must contain 80% butterfat, and most American butters sit right on that cut-off point, whereas most European butters have at least 82% butterfat. Of course, 2% is not a huge discrepancy, unless you're a Michelin-starred pastry chef, so the main difference lies in the nuances of flavour. Butter is butter, after all.

Mantequilla de pobre Another butter that is not technically butter. Mantequilla de pobre translates as 'poor man's butter' and refers to smashed avocados. For much of history, butter has been prohibitively expensive in Central and South America, as dairy farming is not undertaken on the same scale as it is across North America and Europe. However, ripe avocados are plentiful (I read that in Trinidad it is very normal to have an avocado tree in your back garden and I felt very jealous) and so rather than using butter as a spread, it is much more common to mix soft avocado flesh with salt, pepper and a drizzle of olive oil.

BREAD

The Field Loaf

**The Snapery Bakery's
signature loaf**

This is the signature loaf from The Snapery Bakery, and was the first loaf I experimented with at home, when I was still just baking for friends and family. It's inspired by the smell of the fields around my childhood home. It creates a lovely, comforting bread with a very crisp crust and an open fluffy crumb – so it can be used for mopping up all kinds of unctuous sauces, yet also has the integrity needed for a great sandwich.

Making a good sourdough loaf is a lengthy process: you'll bake the loaf the day after you make the dough. Flour strength, temperature and humidity will all affect your dough, so allow plenty of time to experiment and don't be disheartened if it doesn't come out quite right first time. A valuable tip is to bake it for longer than you think it needs – you don't have to worry about it drying out, and a darker crust has much more flavour.

With a bit of practice, it quickly becomes a habit and is such a rewarding skill to master. Soon you'll be able to tear off great hunks of beautiful bread and dip and mop to your heart's content. **RS**

Makes 2
large loaves

A note on the method
For detailed information on the terms and processes used in this recipe, see page 76–82

Equipment
(see also the detailed equipment section on page 83)
very large bowl or plastic container (able to hold 4 litres/4 quarts)
couple of clean tea towels
plastic dough scraper
metal dough scraper (also called a bench knife, you can also use your plastic one)
couple of proving baskets, or large mixing bowls lined with tea towels
Dutch oven combo cooker, or a heavy cast-iron pot with a lid
lame (razor-blade holder) or a very sharp knife

Ingredients
For the leaven
20g (¾oz) sourdough starter (page 76)
40g (1½oz) strong wholemeal (wholewheat) flour
40g (1½oz) strong white flour
80g (3oz) warm water (26–30°C/79–86°F)

For the dough
610g (1lb 5½oz) warm water (26–30°C/79–86°F)
120g (4oz) strong wholemeal flour
680g (1lb 8oz) strong white flour
16g (½oz) sea salt
rice flour, for dusting

Stage 1 Prepare the leaven

Either make a starter from scratch one week before you intend to bake, or use a mature starter if you have a healthy one bubbling away.

In a small pot with a lid – a jam jar is perfect – mix the starter, flours and warm water. Leave in a warm place for 3–4 hours until there are lots of little bubbles and it smells mildly fermented. If you like your bread on the sour side, leave for a further 1–2 hours.

You can also make a leaven the day before you want to make your dough. In that case, once the leaven ingredients are combined, leave at room temperature for 1–2 hours until signs of fermentation appear (tiny bubbles and a slight increase in size), then refrigerate overnight.

Stage 2 Make the dough

Next, weigh 560g (1lb 3½oz) of the warm water into your large bowl or plastic container and add 160g (5½oz) of your leaven. Combine with your fingers, then add both flours and mix until there are no more lumps.

Cover with a clean tea towel and leave to rest for 30–45 minutes: aim for 30 minutes on a warmer day (above 25°C/77°F), and 45 minutes on colder days. Once the dough has rested, add the salt and the remaining 50g (1¾oz) of water. Using your hands, scrunch the salt and water into the dough for about 3–5 minutes until the water is completely absorbed – there should be no visible liquid. Leave the dough to rest, covered, for 30 minutes.

Stage 3 Stretch and fold, and bulk rise

Now, you've probably noticed that there hasn't been anything that resembles traditional kneading, and that's because this method requires no kneading. Sourdough takes a long time to prove compared to yeasted bread and, over the course of the bulk rise, gluten is developed naturally using a 'stretch and fold' technique. Honestly, we don't need kneading; plus, it's knackering.

Once you've added salt to your dough and allowed it to rest, you can start stretching and folding. Wet your hands (this helps to stop the dough sticking) and, keeping the dough in its container, imagine the dough is a clockface. Starting at 12 o'clock, scoop your hands underneath the dough, then pull up (stretch) and fold down (fold) over the whole piece. Turn your container 90° and repeat this step (stretch, fold and turn) another three times, so you end up back where you started. You can even put a small sticker on the outside of your container to help you remember your starting point.

These four folds are considered one 'turn'. After completing the first turn, cover the dough. Then uncover and turn it every 30 minutes for 2–3 hours. After these 4–6 turns, the dough should have changed from loose and stretchy and should have begun to firm, tighten and contain plenty of air bubbles and have risen to nearly twice the size. It's amazing to build such strength in a dough without kneading or a mixer.

Stage 4 Pre-shape

Now your dough is ready to divide and pre-shape which will build a little more strength before the final shaping. After the final turn, rest the dough for 20–30 minutes. Lightly dust the top of the dough with flour and, using a plastic dough scraper, gently coax it away from the edges of the container. Then turn the container upside down and wait for the dough to naturally release itself onto your (unfloured) work surface.

continued >>

Bake it for longer than you think it needs, you don't need to be scared that it will dry out...

Divide the dough into two equal parts using a metal scraper. Put one piece aside while you focus on the other.

Fold the bottom of the dough over the top so it is now floured on the top and bottom. At this point you shouldn't need to use any more flour – you don't want to the dough to slide around on the surface. Holding your scraper in one hand, work the dough into a round, tucking the sides of the dough underneath itself and tightening the surface until it's smooth and bouncy. With practice, you should be able to do this in about three movements, but it might take a little longer to begin with. The idea is to build tension as the dough anchors itself to the table. You need to build strength within the dough – but if the dough tears, you've gone too far. If this happens, just leave the dough to rest for about 10 minutes and then pre-shape again.

Repeat with the other piece of dough, then cover both with a clean tea towel and leave to rest for 20 minutes.

Stage 5 Final shape and retarding
After resting, lightly flour the surface of both pieces of dough and flip them over so the floured side is on the worktop. Thinking of your dough as a clockface again, take hold of the edge of the dough at 2 o'clock and fold it into the middle, securing it with the thumb of your other hand. Rotate the dough about 30° and again fold the 2 o'clock edge to the middle, securing with your thumb.

Repeat this process until you have rotated the dough through 360°. It should feel strong and bouncy and have noticeable resistance to the pressure of your hands. Now you have a ball, flip it over so the smooth side is facing up. Cup your hand round the ball and pull towards you, so that the anchoring dough 'seals' itself. Now you have a fully shaped loaf! Repeat for the other loaf (doing everything twice is great practice and helps you to learn more quickly).

Dust your proving baskets or tea-towel-lined bowls with rice flour (or some strong white flour), then place your loaves in them with their rough sides facing up. Cover with a tea towel, leave to prove in a warm place for 1 hour and then refrigerate overnight; the loaves will be ready to bake first thing in the morning. This process is called 'retarding': slowing down the proving will give you a far superior flavour. (You could just leave your loaves to prove for around 4 hours at warm room temperature – about 25°C/77°F – and bake them when they have almost doubled in size, but that way they will only have a hint of background sourness, if any.)

Stage 6 Bake
When you're ready to bake, put your Dutch oven (or cast-iron pot) in the oven and preheat to 250°C (480°F). If your oven's maximum temperature is lower than that, then just whack it up as high as it will go. Temperature is very important here, if it is not hot enough then your loaves will not get the desired 'spring'.

Take one loaf out of the fridge and turn it out into the Dutch oven, being careful not to burn yourself – cast iron really holds heat and will inflict one hell of a burn. Holding your lame (or very sharp knife) at a 30° angle, make four shallow slashes in the top of the loaf, in a criss-cross or other pattern, then cover with the lid and place in the oven. Turn the temperature down to 220°C (425°F) after 10 minutes, then remove the lid after another 10 minutes – you should be greeted by a huge cloud of steam and a glorious smell. Bake (lid off) for another 20–25 minutes until dark golden brown, and you are done. Take the loaf out of its baking vessel and leave on a windowsill to entice your neighbours. Repeat with the second loaf.

Baking essentials

Starter and leaven

A sourdough starter is a stable culture of natural yeasts and lactic bacteria working in symbiosis. The natural yeast in a culture produces carbon dioxide (CO_2) when it eats the sugars made from the broken down starch. The CO_2 then fills the dough with gas, making it light and sometimes holey, while the lactic bacteria contributes to the characteristic sour flavour.

I use the words starter and leaven to refer to a sourdough culture at different stages. I use a proportion of very mature culture, which I call the 'starter', to make the leaven. A mature starter smells heavily fermented, almost alcoholic, tastes citric and looks almost fizzy.

To make the leaven (the more mild culture) from this, I add flour and water. The leaven is used to make the dough, and is used at a much 'younger' stage, when it smells mild and tastes mildly lactic, like yogurt.

You may consider it weird to be tasting this swamp-like porridge, but it's the best way to get to know your culture. You'll remember the taste when it is happy and when it is a little under the weather.

Making a sourdough starter

To begin with it is quite a lengthy procedure (6 or 7 days), but once you have a stable starter, you can make bread every day. The key to success is patience and belief. Don't give up. If it takes 3 days to show signs of fermentation, that's OK.

To make a sourdough starter that can successfully leaven dough, you need to promote the growth of natural yeast. Natural yeast is abundant all around us, and is especially abundant in flour.

Our starter at The Snapery was initially mixed with Ukrainian hop flowers that had been rolled in a rye paste and dried. My good friend Olia Hercules brought these back from the Ukraine. The purpose of adding these was to kick-start fermentation. Many people believe that adding raisins or fruit peel can also speed up the process and add character.

After years of baking, I now know that the only catalyst you need is time. And flour and water are all you need to encourage the growth of natural yeast and lactic bacteria.

Starters at different stages of fermentation, from left to right: not enough fizz; perfect fizz; and too much fizz

DAY 1

In a jar, mix 100g (3½oz) warm water with 50g (1¾oz) quality strong white flour and 50g (1¾oz) wholemeal flour. Cover with a wet tea towel and leave in a warm place for 48 hours.

After 48 hours, look for signs of fermentation. There should be a few bubbles on the surface. It might not have any smell at this point, but if it smells vaguely alcoholic then you're on to a winner. It will probably look quite grey, but will be fresh underneath. If there is no sign of any activation, do not worry. Put the jar in a slightly warmer place and leave for a further 24 hours and then continue from 'day 3'.

DAY 3

If you have the beginning of fermentation, great news! You're only a few days away from some exceptional bread. Discard half of the starter and add another 100g (3½oz) warm water with 50g (1¾oz) white flour and 50g (1¾oz) wholemeal flour. Cover and leave in a warm place for another 24 hours.

DAY 4

Repeat the process in 'day 3'. At this point, there should be more obvious signs of fermentation: small bubbles, visual growth in size and a slight tang on the nose.

DAY 5

Repeat the discarding and replenishing as in 'day 3'.

DAY 6

You should have something that's almost ready to use in a bread recipe. The colour should be similar to the colour it was when you mixed it. There should be a lot of bubbles, quite an alcoholic smell and it should have grown to almost twice the size. Repeat the discarding and feeding in 'day 3' one more time. After this, it should be ready to use in your bread recipe.

Looking after your starter

The most important thing to remember when maintaining a starter is routine and temperature. This is not an inert object, this is not something you can store in a cupboard and forget about until next you need it. This is a living thing, and like all living things it needs to be treated as such. It needs regular feeding to survive, it needs warmth when required, and if it's feeling lazy, it needs encouragement to give it some get up and go.

Ideally, you feed your starter every day. Maybe twice a day during the summer. Every starter has a slightly different routine and you'll get to know what suits yours over time. It's hard to give specific advice as everyone's house has a different ambient temperature. Just look, smell and taste, and learn what is best. Try to mix the starter so it is 22°C (72°F) and feed at regular intervals.

If you decide that every day is too much commitment, you can choose to store your starter in the fridge for up to a week before feeding. Before you want to make bread I would recommend feeding for 2 days at room temp before adding to a dough to get it back on track as it's likely to be sluggish after sleeping for so long.

To feed the soughdough starter

Measure out 1 tablespoon of your sourdough starter and discard the rest. To the tablespoon of starter, add equal parts water and flour. Use 40g (1½oz) water and 20g (¾oz) strong white flour and 20g (¾oz) wholemeal flour.

The longer you leave the starter to ferment, the more acidic it will become. We use ours after

3–4 hours. Using it at this stage will produce a mildly sour loaf. It's really down to taste. If you like it more sour, 5 or 6 hours (and using slightly colder water) would work better.

After you have used your starter to make the leaven for your dough, you will have roughly 1 tablespoon left. If you used the starter at an acidic stage (6–10 hours), you can feed it again immediately to keep it going for future loaves. If it was used at a mild stage, cover the starter and leave for a couple of hours before feeding.

As mentioned above, if kept in the fridge, the starter can keep for a week and then be revived at room temperature (feed before using), but I'd be cautious about leaving it for longer than that. Regular feeding is the key to a healthy starter.

Know your bread

You may have noticed that the bread recipes are pretty lengthy – the techniques can take practice to get right, so I wanted to put a few notes here to and give some pointers on what to look out for when making bread. The more functional instructions are listed within the Field Loaf recipe on pages 70–75.

What we do at The Snapery Bakery is not to be taken as the only way, but it's the way that works for us. Other bakers might explain the methods slightly differently – or completely differently! But that's what is so fun about being a baker. The way we do it, goes as follows…

Making the leaven and dough
After making the leaven (which can be done in advance), it's simply a case of mixing in the flour and water to create a dough. Well, sort of.

Since yeast is reactive to temperature you will always have to adjust what you do over the seasons. In summer the temperature of the water you'll use will be dramatically different than in winter. In the hottest summer months at The Snapery we use ice-cold water, and in the winter we can use water up to 28°C (82°C). It's important to think about the temperature of your kitchen before you mix your dough.

Generally the flour will be the same temperature as the air. A good way of calculating the temperature of water you need is to note the desired temperature of your dough, then multiply this by 3, then subtract the air and the flour temperature. The figure you're left with is what your water temperature should be. It's not 100% accurate, but it'll get you to within 1 or 2 degrees.

Bulk rise / Stretch and fold

It's important to leave the dough to rise in a mass before dividing. This is called the 'bulk rise'. During this bulk rise, we turn the dough several times in what is called 'stretch and fold'.

This process is a brilliant double act: when you're not stretching and folding the dough, it will be proving. And there's a beautiful relationship between building structure in the dough and the rate at which the dough is proving.

It's easy think that because you've done the amount of folds in the recipe that you're ready to move on to the pre-shape. But learn to read the dough: it's like a ball slowly being filled with gas as the gluten develops and the dough leavens. If you move on to pre-shape before the dough is taut enough, it won't hold its shape. Equally, over-prove it and the ball will burst.

The technique of stretch and fold is an alternative to kneading for wet dough (which is obviously quite difficult to knead). It's really about using time rather than force. The stretch and fold builds gluten (the same as kneading), as well as creating a stronger, more flavourful dough. Recipes that use less water than our recipes will still require kneading, as the gluten cannot build without heavier manipulation. Very wet doughs enhance gluten development as it is easier for the gluten molecules to align and develop a strong gluten network.

Temperature and time is key here. Generally, for us at the bakery, the dough would have almost doubled after 2½–3 hours at 27°C (81°F) after receiving 3–4 'turns'. We use a high power mixer at the bakery, which develops the dough over a short period of time. This means that we don't have to use so many turns.

By hand I would use a dough temperature of 23–24°C (73–75°F) performing 5 or 6 folds every 30 minutes over a 3–4 hour period.

A good indication it is ready is when it has almost doubled, it has a slightly domed surface, if you press the dough with a wet finger it should spring back slowly but feel bouncy, aerated and taut. If it needs longer, the dough will be flat, fairly slack and lifeless. This could indicate that the dough temperature isn't high enough, in which case I would recommend trying a warmer place in your kitchen.

If I need the dough to be warmer at home I use my oven as a proving chamber. With the oven switched off I place a bowl of hot water on the floor and put my dough on the shelf above and close the door. The temperature in the oven will then be roughly about 40°C (104°F), so you can use this chamber until you have achieved the desired dough temperature.

Pre-shaping / Building structure

Stretch and fold is a bit like brickwork, you layer and layer the dough and it becomes stronger and stronger as the gluten develops. The ball becomes almost buoyant. You then need to pre-shape it to build the dough up further. Pre-shaping is essentially forming the dough into a tight ball to give it a regular shape.

One of the reasons for this is so you get a good rise when you bake. If you have a loose flat dough that starts to fill with carbon dioxide, the dough will spread out like a puddly pancake. Whereas if the dough is nice and tight, when it fills with gas, the only way is up. It is like a stretched elastic band... it has power. The elastic band is at its most powerful when stretched out to its absolute limit before breaking. That's what I try and do with dough.

To get maximum lift in the oven it needs to be like that elastic band waiting to ping and fire off. As tight as it can be before it tears.

Final shaping

With the technique in this book, the final shape is fairly unimportant in relation to the previous steps. If all has gone well you would have built a dough with a lot of structure. All that needs to happen at this point it to make it into the shape you want. Usually at home I make a round loaf because I bake in a Dutch oven and use the technique described in the Field Loaf recipe (page 70).

Slash and bake

This is the most fun part. Slashing your loaf and baking. Before you turn your dough out into your pot (Dutch oven) think about how you want to cut it. For me it should be your own, do whatever you like. But classic cuts are a cross, a box, diamond cross hatch and a single cut down the middle.

When cutting, after the dough is turned out into the Dutch oven, make sure the blade is at an acute angle as if almost flat to the surface of the dough. This will dictate which direction the dough will burst open and give you what is known as an 'ear'.

Generally, a loaf of 800g (1lb 12oz) or more should be in the oven for 40–50 minutes in order for it to be fully baked, but if you want a darker crust a few more minutes won't dry out your crumb.

Never cut into a loaf directly from the oven! Warm bread is amazing, but hot bread is no where near as pleasurable. Wait until almost fully cooled before slicing. The crust will be crisp, the crumb very slightly warm so the lashings of butter very slightly melts, then enjoy. Pure joy!

Each time Rich comes home from the bakery, pulls a loaf out of a brown paper bag and cuts me a slice, it never fails to astound me that this shiny, bubbly, tangy loaf has been made with just three ingredients. EH

Equipment

Digital scales To make sure you are as accurate as possible, use digital.

Large mixing bowl or plastic container
It makes a difference if the container used for mixing and proving your dough is quite full or not. If it is too big, it becomes easier for the dough to relax and flatten. For the Field Loaf recipe, a 5–7 litre- (5–7 quart-) plastic container or mixing bowl is perfect.

Temperature probe One of the most important pieces of equipment a baker can own. Everyone will consider 'warm' water to be a different temperature. I'm very specific with temperature in this book, and that is because every degree counts. One degree can be the difference of up to 1 hour in proving time. It's useful to take the temperature in lots of different places in your kitchen to survey the micro-climate. You'll get to know where to sit your dough if you need it to be somewhere a little warmer or cooler. It's also useful to take a temperature reading every time you turn your dough in order to maintain the desired temperature. You'll become obsessed with it… It's fun!

Dough scrapers Use plastic for releasing dough from containers, and metal scrapers (known also as a bench knife or scotch scraper) for dividing and handling dough.

Baking cloth or tea towel and linen couche
Baking cloth or clean tea towels are ideal for covering dough. We use what's called a 'couche' for proving baguettes and occasionally loaves. If made from untreated flax linen, they cannot be machine washed due to shrinkage. We simply brush our linen clean everyday. If you get dough stuck to your couche, let it dry and scrape it off with a metal scraper.

Banneton (proving basket) There are many different types of banneton. They are traditionally made from wicker, but can be made from wood pulp, rattan or plastic. Many wicker baskets will be lined with natural linen, which the dough is much less likely to stick to. We prefer a wood pulp basket. You can also use a large mixing bowl lined with a tea towel.

Dutch oven or heavy cast-iron pot Most food lovers will have a heavy cast-iron pot. These are ideal to bake in. The idea is to bake with the lid on to trap the steam which gives the loaf a much better rise – a moist environment means the crust won't set too early. The loaf is then baked further with the lid removed to allow the loaf to colour. At home I have a Dutch oven combo cooker. You can use it either way up as the lid also acts as a shallow skillet. I turn the dough out into the skillet and slash, then use the large pot as a lid. It's a lot easier to cut when you don't have to reach into a scorching hot pot. I've had many a burn. If you want to invest in a dedicated baking pot, I recommend a Lodge Dutch oven combo cooker. Well worth it.

Baking stone You can use a stone for baguettes or loaves. Don't buy a thin cheap pizza stone, they are useless. Go for a thick piece of granite. Something you can barely lift!

Peel This is a paddle-shaped piece of wood and is what we use to slide baguettes or loaves directly onto a hot stone in the oven. They're easy to find from any baking website, or any piece of appropriately sized wood will do.

Lame (razor blade holder) This is used to cut the top of the loaf before baking. You can buy specific holders for the blades, but some people just use a thin piece of metal.

The Field Loaf
Variations

Once you have mastered a great sourdough, a very simple trick to increase your bread repertoire is to add different ingredients, creating new flavours and textures. Keep in mind that these additions will change the dough significantly, so it's not just a case of popping a few olives in and calling it a new loaf. You still have to learn how the dough reacts to each addition, and The Field Loaf recipe (page 70) is perfect for experimenting with to discover the different properties of the resulting loaves.

For example, the Sunflower, Flax & Honey Loaf has a magnificent brittle crunch that is delicious with hard, salty cheeses and sweet, sticky membrillo. This is created in two ways: firstly, the seeds used to coat the loaf draw moisture from the dough to crisp the crust; and secondly, the seeds release gums when they are hydrated, and these become firm and crisp when dry. **RS**

These are some of our favourite loaves from the bakery, from top to bottom: Olive & Rosemary Loaf; Sunflower, Flax & Honey Loaf; and Polenta, Cheddar & Jalapeño Loaf

Polenta, Cheddar & Jalapeño Loaf

Ingredients

For the polenta
250g (9oz) vegetable stock (or
  125g/4½oz buttermilk and
  125g/4½oz water)
60g (2oz) polenta
1 sprig thyme, leaves picked
15g (½oz) butter
25g (1oz) Parmesan,
  finely grated
sea salt and freshly ground
  black pepper

For the dough
1 x Field Loaf dough (page 70)
50g (1¾oz) mature cheddar,
  grated
50g (1¾oz) pickled jalapeños,
  sliced

First, cook the polenta. In a medium pan over a medium heat bring the stock (or buttermilk and water) to a simmer and sprinkle in the polenta, stirring constantly. Add the thyme leaves to the polenta mix, then generously season with salt and pepper.

Cook, stirring continuously, until the polenta is stiff, roughly 15 minutes. Then stir in the butter and Parmesan and leave to cool.

Following the Field Loaf recipe (page 70), make your basic dough. At the end of Stage 2, rest the dough for 15 minutes (rather than the stated 30 minutes).

Next, add the cooked polenta, the cheddar and jalapeños to the dough. Break up the polenta, then squidge and fold it into the dough until roughly combined.

Then continue to follow the Field Loaf method from Stage 3 onwards. Do note, as the dough will be fairly taut, don't worry about getting a perfectly smooth dough. Just believe that over the course of between 3–6 'turns', your dough will become beautifully silky… and will smell phenomenal.

Sunflower, Flax & Honey Loaf

Ingredients
1 x Field Loaf dough (page 70)
1 tablespoon cold-pressed
  sunflower oil
35g (1½oz) honey
125g (4½oz) sunflower seeds
60g (2oz) flaxseeds

Following the Field Loaf recipe (page 70), make your basic dough. At the end of Stage 2, rest the dough for 15 minutes (rather than the stated 30 minutes).

Next, add the sunflower oil, honey, 65g (2¼oz) of the sunflower seeds and 35g (1¼oz) of the flaxseeds. Incorporate with your hands until roughly mixed.

Then continue with the Field Loaf method to the end of Stage 5 when you have final shaped loaves ready to be put in the baskets to prove. Put the remaining seeds in a large, shallow dish. Very lightly brush or spray water onto the smooth side of the loaves, then gently press each one into the seeds (smooth side down) to coat the crust – the water helps the seeds to stick.

Follow the remaining stages of the Field Loaf method.

Olive & Rosemary Loaf

Ingredients
1 x Field Loaf dough (page 70)
200g (7oz) manzanilla olives,
  pitted and roughly chopped
7 sprigs rosemary (3 of the
  sprigs finely chopped)
25g (1oz) extra virgin olive oil

Following the Field Loaf recipe (page 70), make your basic dough. At the end of Stage 2, rest the dough for 15 minutes (rather than the stated 30 minutes).

Add the olives, chopped rosemary and the olive oil to the dough, then use your hands to incorporate.

Then continue to follow the remaining stages of the Field Loaf method – but, before you 'retard' the dough, line each proving basket with 2 sprigs of rosemary, to decorate the top of the loaf when it is turned out after baking.

New York Deli Loaf

I visited NYC ten years ago and immediately wanted to live there, for one main reason: the Reuben sandwich. The sights of the city occupied us, but we were really just waiting for the next sandwich opportunity, in between the inspiring architecture and unique cultural landmarks. We took the ferry to Staten Island, a horse-drawn ride around Central Park, and we saw Times Square. We also went to a lot of dive bars and hung out in Brooklyn – but by far my favourite thing about New York was the seemingly endless number of tiny delis, cafés and diners hidden away from the (other) tourists. I still salivate at the thought of those sandwiches: pastrami, sauerkraut, Emmental, pickles, all on rye.

So, naturally, at the bakery we needed to make a loaf that could handle a pound of pastrami. We weren't out to recreate something; we would put our own spin on it and make it naturally leavened. Thinking about the bread's Jewish European roots, we'd also add a hint of caraway – and, of course, use rye flour.

Just imagine yourself, early in the morning, feeling proud of your latest baking experiment, when you turn to your fellow baker and ask, 'Who's got the pastrami?' Silence. The perfect loaf for a Reuben, but no Reuben to be had. What followed was the least-appreciated sausage and mustard sandwich I've ever eaten. The lesson here: never forget the pastrami. **RS**

<u>Makes 2</u>
<u>large loaves</u>

Ingredients
For the leaven
20g (¾oz) sourdough starter
  (page 76)
80g (3oz) strong white flour
80g (3oz) warm water
  (26–30°C/79–86°F)

For the dough
760g (1lb 10½oz) strong
  white flour
40g (1½oz) dark rye flour
650g (1lb 7oz) warm water
  (26–30°C/79–86°F)
16g (½oz) caraway seeds
14g (½oz) sea salt

Ideally you would use an all-white-flour sourdough starter for this recipe. Don't worry too much if you only have a wholemeal-and-white-flour starter; just use what you have – when it's mixed with the flour and water for the leaven, the bran content will be negligible.

Combine the leaven ingredients in a bowl and leave at room temperature for 1–2 hours until signs of fermentation appear (tiny bubbles and a slight increase in size), then refrigerate overnight – or you can use it the same day if a teaspoon of the leaven floats when dropped into some water.

To make the dough, put both flours, 590g (1lb 4½oz) of the water and 160g (6oz) of the leaven into a large bowl and mix by hand for about 5 minutes until you have a rough dough with no lumps of flour. Cover and rest for 30 minutes.

Add the remaining water, together with the caraway seeds and salt, and incorporate by giving the dough a good old scrunch and pummel (taking fistfuls of the dough and rapidly squeezing it in your fists) for about 5 minutes, or until smooth and all the water has been absorbed.

Leave to rest for 30 minutes, then follow the Field Loaf method (page 73) from Stage 3 onwards. And whatever you do, do not forget the pastrami.

<u>The majority of the recipes in this book use a sourdough starter made from wholemeal and white flour. This loaf calls for an all-white-flour sourdough starter.</u>

The Heritage Loaf

For farmers to survive today, they choose to grow the safest grains. This usually means wheat varieties with a high yield and high tolerance to pests, making them cheaper to produce. Heritage grains (more common before the Industrial Revolution) generally have taller stalks and smaller grains, which are harder to harvest. They also grow more slowly, meaning they're less economically viable for many farmers.

Ten years ago, heritage grains were prohibitively expensive. More recently however, consumer demand has made them more affordable and a wider variety of grains are now readily available. Slowly but surely, the tides are turning, and each week people ask me about the grains we're using, spurring us on to experiment and see what else we can bake. This means we are getting to use some exciting grains, some of which were first cultivated over 20,000 years ago.

This loaf is one of my all-time favourites, the emmer (also known as farro) really makes it something special. The dough is silky and easy to shape, despite being quite hydrated. It produces a loaf with an open crumb and a crust as crisp as they come. Eat with strong blue cheese and a glass of chilled Riesling. **RS**

Makes 2 large loaves

Ingredients
For the leaven
20g (¾oz) sourdough starter using all-white flour (page 76)
80g (3oz) strong white flour
80g (3oz) warm water (26–30°C/79–86°F)

For the dough
480g (1lb 1oz) strong white flour
240g (8½oz) wholemeal (wholewheat) spelt flour
100g (3½oz) wholemeal (wholewheat) emmer flour
640g (1lb 7oz) warm water (26–30°C/79–86°F)
19g (¾oz) sea salt

Follow the Field Loaf method (page 73), using the leaven ingredients and flour blend listed here, and with the addition of 1 or 2 more 'turns' at Stage 3.

As these grains have a lower protein content than standard wheat, the extra turns are required to strengthen the dough and give it that typical sourdough structure. Using wholegrain flour means that you need the extra water to open out the texture of the loaf. The dough will also rise less, making the final loaf a little broader and flatter than the Field Loaf, so don't be alarmed if this loaf isn't as voluminous as some of your other ones.

Baguettes

Baguettes are among the most satisfying breads to make. The method is a little tricky to master at first, but when your baguettes are looking pretty with their waves of 'ears' all lined up, you get an enormous sense of achievement – one I feel (almost) every day at work. (Of course, no one is perfect, and we still screw up now and then!) This recipe is adapted from a very traditional French baguette recipe. I've reduced the hydration slightly to make it easier while you're getting to grips with the technique. You may also find it useful to consult YouTube or Google if you're struggling to visualise the exact action needed at any stage. **RS**

Makes 5–6 baguettes

Equipment
*(see also the detailed equipment
    section on page 83)*
very large bowl or plastic container
    (able to hold 4 litres/4 quarts)
couple of clean tea towels
plastic dough scraper
metal dough scraper (also called
    a bench knife, you can also use
    your plastic one)
linen couche or 3 clean
    tea towels
baking stone or heavy
    baking tray
roasting tin
peel and flipping board
lame (razor-blade holder) or a very
    sharp knife

Ingredients
For the leaven
20g (¾oz) sourdough starter
    (page 76)
80g (3oz) strong white flour
80g (3oz) warm water (26–30°C/79–86°F)

For the dough
800g (1lb 12oz) T65 French baguette
    flour (or white flour with 11–12%
    protein content – it should say
    on the packet)
2g (½ teaspoon) instant dried yeast
580g (1lb 4½oz) warm water
    (23°C/73°F)
17g (½oz) sea salt
rice flour or fine semolina, for dusting

continued >>

Start by making the leaven by following Stage 1 on page 73.

Put the flour, leaven, yeast and 540g (1lb 3½oz) of the water into a large bowl. Bring the dough together using your hands and work until smooth, roughly 5 minutes.

Rest, uncovered, for 30 minutes at room temperature.

Once rested, add the salt and the rest of the water. Scrunch the salt in with your hands (take fistfuls of the dough and squeeze it) until the salt and water are all incorporated, then work it (knead) in the bowl for a further 3–4 minutes to strengthen the dough.

Rest again, covered in the bowl, for 30 minutes at room temperature.

Perform the Stage 3 'stretch and fold' technique on page 73. Complete 3–4 'turns' (rather than 4–6), until the dough feels springy and has almost doubled in size.

Now it's time for the pre-shape. Flour the top of your dough and gently coax it away from the sides of the bowl with a dough scraper. Hold the bowl upside down over a clean work surface and let the dough naturally fall out. Flour the top of the dough and then lightly flatten it by pressing down gently with your hands to release a little of the gas. Divide it into 5–6 neat 250–300g (9–10½oz) rectangles, each roughly 18cm x 10cm (7in x 4in).

Place one of the rectangles horizontally in front of you, with the shorter ends pointing to 3 o'clock and 9 o'clock, then take the bottom left-hand corner diagonally up to the middle, about a quarter of the way up the rectangle,

and push down to secure. Mirror with the bottom right-hand corner, then gently roll the dough up and away from you to make a cylindrical shape. This is your pre-shaped baguette. Set aside on your work surface, then repeat with the rest of the dough.

Cover your pre-shaped baguettes with a clean tea towel – you should have 5 or 6. Leave to rest for 30 minutes.

Now you can either move on to the final shaping and baking, or store the pre-shaped baguettes in a container overnight in the fridge, ready to be finished in the morning.

Line a baking sheet or a wooden board with a linen couche or tea towel and dust with rice flour or semolina. Flour the tops of your pre-shaped baguettes. Then, using a metal scraper, flip one of them over so the floured side is now resting on the surface.

Working with the baguette horizontally in front of you, with the ends pointing to 3 o'clock and 9 o'clock, fold the top of the dough down leaving a gap of about 2½cm (1in) along the bottom. Press gently to secure all the way along. Turn the dough 180° and repeat, then turn through 180° and repeat again.

Next, you need to seal the baguette into a long cylindrical shape. Starting at one end, take hold of the top of the dough and join it to the bottom, using the heel of your hand to firmly seal the edges of the dough together, but being careful not to squish the main body of the dough. Moving gradually along the length of the baguette until the whole baguette has been sealed and it vaguely resembles a fat baguette (the sealed side of your baguette is called the 'seam') – see the top left picture.

continued >>

>>

Now you need to elongate and taper the baguette at each end. Starting in the middle, place both your hands over the baguette so that both your fingertips and the heels of your hands are touching the work surface. Adjust the height of your hands to apply gentle pressure on the baguette, but do not squash. Gently roll back and forth while moving your hands outwards to stretch the dough. Do this a couple of times if necessary, until your baguette is the desired length (bearing in mind the depth and width of your oven!). On your last roll, tilt the outer edge of your palms down towards the work surface at each end of the baguette to taper – I like mine dangerously pointy.

Place your fully shaped baguette, seam-side up, on your couche or tea towel and tuck up some of the material on either side of it to make a pleat roughly 4cm (1½in) taller than your baguette. Shape another baguette, making another pleat next to it and checking there's enough rice flour so the baguettes don't stick to the couche. When all the baguettes are in the couche, prove for 1–1½ hours until they have risen just to the top of the pleats. When they're ready, the dough should spring back slowly (about 2 seconds) if you press it with your finger.

Place a baking stone or heavy baking sheet on the middle shelf of your oven and a roasting tin on the bottom shelf, then preheat to 250°C (480°F) or as high as it will go. The journey is nearly over for your lovely little baguettes. In the bakery we use something called a peel (a large flat board with a handle) to slide the baguettes. We load up the peel with loaves and then slide them off, directly – and sometimes gracefully – onto the stone floor of the oven. You can buy peels, but if you have some thin untreated wood, that will do just fine; a large, rimless baking sheet, or even a sheet of stiff

cardboard will do the job too. You'll also need a long, thin piece of wood or cardboard, roughly 40cm x 8cm x ½cm (16in x 3in x ¼in), to use as a flipping board. The more punk, the better! (If you don't have anything appropriate to hand, it's OK – you'll just have to be as quick and gentle as possible…)

Dust the baguettes with rice flour and very gently pull the couche at one end to create a little space between the first pleat and the first baguette. Holding the flipping board in your good hand and the end of the couche in the other, nestle the board between the pleat and the baguette. Now pull the couche so it is taut but not disturbing the other baguettes and roll the baguette onto its seam side.

Shuffle the baguette, seam-side down, onto your peel or makeshift peel. Flip as many baguettes onto the peel as will fit, leaving at least 6cm (2½in) between each one. (If you find you need to bake them in two batches, keep the still-couched baguettes in a cool place or the fridge until you're ready for them.)

Baguettes need several slashes to achieve their classic look. As I understand it, a traditional baguette should have five slashes, but this really depends on the length of your baguette. To get what we call 'ears' (where the dough bursts through where you have cut to create beautiful waves), you cut at an angle, almost as if you were trying to skin the baguette. Working horizontally, imagine there is a 2cm (¾in) stripe running along the length of the baguette, straight down the middle. Take your lame/blade and turn it towards you until it's almost flat. Starting at the left end of the baguette (if you're right handed), make a shallow and decisive cut about 6cm (2½in) long, from the top to the bottom of your imaginary stripe.

The next cut will again start at the top of this stripe, its starting point overlapping the first cut by a quarter. As most domestic ovens aren't very deep, your baguettes won't be a traditional size, therefore you'll likely only manage to slash the baguette two or three times, but if you can do more then give it go.

When you're ready to bake, open the oven door and pour about 250g (9oz) boiling water into the roasting tin at the bottom of the oven to generate steam (this is vital for the final rise in the oven, and will also give an attractive shine to the baked baguettes).

Quickly and confidently, slide your baguettes onto the hot baking stone or baking sheet and swiftly shut the oven door to trap as much steam as possible. Bake for 15–18 minutes until the colour of gold. Now you are almost French. Congratulations!

Buttermilk Rye Bread

Makes 2 small loaves

Equipment
plastic dough scraper
2 x 500g (1lb) loaf tins

Ingredients
For the leaven
20g (¾oz) sourdough starter
(page 76)
60g (2oz) strong white flour
60g (2oz) strong wholemeal
(wholewheat) flour
120g (4oz) warm water
(26–30°C/79–86°F)

For the dough
200g (7oz) Cultured Buttermilk
(page 140), at warm room
temperature (25°C/77°F)
40g (1½oz) clear honey
220g (7¾oz) warm water
(30°C/86°F)
400g (14oz) dark rye flour,
extra for dusting
40g (1½oz) pumpkin seeds
30g (1oz) linseeds
8g (¼oz) sea salt

Rye bread is an intriguing thing. You can't treat the dough like a typical bread dough, as it has the consistency of stiff concrete. No stretch and fold, or slap and fold, or fold and fold. Due to the very low gluten content of rye flour, there is no elasticity in it, so we can't rely on any of the things we've learnt about bread-making.

This was our first rye bread at The Snapery Bakery. It was a very long time in the making and in the end was achieved by encouraging the bakers to forget everything they thought they knew about bread. **RS**

continued >>

The day before you want to bake your loaves, make your leaven by following the Stage 1 instructions on page 73. Leave the leaven at room temperature until tiny bubbles appear, then refrigerate overnight.

The next day, mix the buttermilk, honey and 200g (7oz) of the water with the leaven until combined, then add the flour and seeds and mix by hand until smooth.

Leave to rest for 30 minutes. Grease the loaf tins with butter.

Add the salt and remaining water to the dough and scrunch with your hands until they are completely absorbed.

Using a wet hand, smooth over the surface of the dough, then dust liberally with rye flour. Prove, uncovered, for 1–2 hours until the surface of the dough resembles a cracked pavement.

The shaping process for this bread is very different to the other breads in this book: using a plastic scraper, scoop half the dough onto a floured surface. Lightly dust the sticky top of the dough with rye flour and pat it into a long rectangle. As gently as you can, roll up the dough into a cylinder and, using your scraper, place it into a greased 500g (1lb) loaf tin. Repeat with the remaining dough.

Using a wet plastic dough scraper, neaten the loaves to make sure that they're snug in their tins, then dust heavily with rye flour.

Prove in a warm place (25–30°C/77–86°F) for 1½–2 hours until the surface of the dough looks like a dried-up watering hole.

Preheat the oven to 225°C (435°F). Place a roasting tin on the bottom shelf of the oven and fill with 250g (9oz) of just-boiled water. Bake the loaves for 45 minutes until nice and dark. The smell of this bread coming out of the oven always blows us away in the bakery.

Turn out and cool on a wire rack. Do not be tempted to cut into it right away, as it will likely still be a little stodgy in the middle. I think this loaf is at its best when it has fully cooled and can be sliced and turned into a delicious smörgås (open sandwich) topped with pastrami and pickles.

The shaping process here is very different to other breads – it's so wet and cement-like, the shaping can seem impossible.

Beer Bread

I first got asked to make a beer sourdough loaf for a surprise birthday party for my friend. Wheat beer seemed like the obvious choice, so I bought some Hoegarden as it was the only one at the local shop, and still a decent quality beer. At first I thought that maybe three-quarters of the liquid amount in the recipe would yield an intensely floral and possibly unpalatable flavour. The next day, during the bake, the bakery smelt more like a brewery, and my mind turned to the poor party guests who would have to suffer beer in solid form. Pulling the loaves from the oven, I was extremely happy with how they looked: dark and shiny, due to the additional sugar in the beer. An hour or so later, it was time for the taste test. Had I captured essence of the pub? Or would it be Golden Glory? It seems obvious now, but because both of the main ingredients in the dough and in the beer were wheat, the flavour of the beer was almost untraceable and it just tasted like a lovely regular sourdough with an immensely crispy crust. Having been so sceptical about the whole thing, I took this as a victory, and decided that the next time I made some bread with beer I'd make it a more unusual one.

At The Snapery Bakery, we're surrounded by an ever-increasing number of breweries. On a Saturday, they open their doors to the public, forming what's come to be known as the Bermondsey Beer Mile. I've heard it's very hard to complete without falling over, but it's an incredible scene and I'm very grateful to be around it. What with all this beer on my doorstep, I decided only local would do. And with the elusive flavour of my last attempt in mind, I went for possibly the most unusual that Bermondsey has to offer. Hiver beer is made using honey harvested from rooftop hives by Bermondsey Street Bees – that's a whole lotta Bermondsey in a bottle! Blonde and malty, with a honeyed finish: delicious, and perfect for my baking needs.

With a beer as distinctive as this, I left the ratio of beer to water the same, and added some chopped malted rye grain to turbocharge the flavour even further. There's a lot of additional flavours here, so this bread differs from a lot of the other recipes in that it is made mainly with white flour. This time the aromas in the bakery were of malt and honey, and I was sure we were onto a winner. When it emerged from the oven, the crust was as golden as the sun and the smell made it near-impossible to resist cutting straight into it. We managed 30 minutes before slicing it: all the flavours were present, but not overpowering. This is a handsome loaf for meaty dinners, but also a surprisingly versatile breakfast bread. **RS**

Makes 2 loaves

Ingredients
For the leaven
20g (¾oz) sourdough starter
  (page 76)
80g (3oz) warm water
  (26°C/79°F)
80g (3oz) strong white flour

For the dough
800g (1lb 12oz) strong
  white flour
40g (1½oz) chopped malted
  rye grain
420g (14¾oz) warm beer
  (26°C/79°F)
220g (8oz) warm water
  (26°C/79°F)
16g (½oz) sea salt

Mix the leaven ingredients. Leave at room temperature for 1–2 hours until signs of fermentation appear (tiny bubbles and a slight increase in size), then refrigerate overnight – or you can use it the same day if a teaspoon of the leaven floats when dropped into some water.

Put the flour, rye grain, beer, 170g (6oz) of the water and 160g (5½oz) of the leaven into a large bowl. (There should be about 20g (¾oz) leaven left for you to refresh and reuse.) Mix by hand until fully combined and there are no visible lumps of flour. Rest for 30 minutes.

Once rested, add the salt and the remaining water and combine until completely smooth and all the moisture has been absorbed.

Follow the Field Loaf method (page 73) from Stage 3.

Nordic Fjellbrød

In 2016, Eve and I decided to flee the inescapable disappointment of New Year's Eve by taking a well-timed break in Norway. The imminent threat of organised fun was happily quashed by our new-found appreciation for fjords, mountains and plentiful fish. Of course, I was also interested in what the country had to offer in the world of bread. We soon discovered that Norwegian bakers use a lot of spelt and, as you might expect in Scandinavia, a lot of rye.

After sampling many loaves, it was the spelty ones that piqued my curiosity. As far as I could tell, they were made using the same process as rye bread, with the addition of lots of whole grains. There was also a mild tang and a slight sweetness, which gave my brain the sweet-and-sour hit it always craves. I wanted to make bread like this.

Back in London, I set about trying to recreate a bread that would remind me of the great times we'd had in Bergen and Oslo. But first I needed to find an authentic rye bread recipe to base my spelt version on. One of my friends, Caecilie Hougaard Pedersen, runs a pop-up Danish food business. She uses her mother's rye bread recipe for her open sandwiches, so I asked her if I could use it as a starting point. I was relieved that she was happy to share, and this gave me the knowledge I needed to start experimenting. After switching some grains, seeds and flour, I finally managed to unearth the memories and flavours of those loaves we had bought in Norway, one cold New Year's Eve. **RS**

**Makes 3 small
or 2 large loaves**

Equipment
very large bowl or plastic
   container (able to hold
   4 litres/4 quarts)
plastic dough scraper
metal dough scraper (also called
   a bench knife, you can also
   use your plastic one)
3 x 500g (1lb) or 2 x 900g
   (2lb) loaf tins
roasting tin

Ingredients
Wet ingredients
250g (9oz) rye leaven (see
   method, right)
500g (1lb 2oz) warm water
   (26–30°C/79–86°F)
125g (4½oz) whole rye grains
125g (4½oz) whole spelt grains
125g (4½oz) pumpkin seeds
30g (1oz) barley malt syrup,
   black treacle or honey

For the dough
500g (1lb 2oz) wholemeal
   (wholewheat) spelt flour,
   extra for dusting
15g (½oz) sea salt
rye flour, for dusting

This recipe uses a rye leaven. If
you don't already have one, take
1 tablespoon of mature sourdough
starter (page 76) and add it to 125g
(4½oz) warm water (30–35°C/86–95°F)
and 125g (4½oz) rye flour. Leave to
ferment until lots of small bubbles
appear, roughly 1½–2½ hours.

The day before you want to bake,
make the rye leaven by mixing all the
wet ingredients together in a large
bowl. Cover and leave to stand at
room temperature for about an hour,
then refrigerate overnight.

The next day, you should have
something that resembles stagnant
pond water. Delicious! Leave it in
a warm place (25–30°C/77–86°F)
to come to room temperature
(23–25°C/73–77°F).

Add the wholemeal spelt flour to this
mixture and combine by hand for
about 5 minutes until there are no
lumps of flour.

Rest for 30 minutes. Meanwhile,
grease the loaf tins with butter.

When the dough has rested, scrunch
in the salt with your hands. Really
scrunch it! When it's fully incorporated,
dust the top of the dough with spelt
flour and prove, uncovered, for 1–2
hours until the floury top has a lovely
pavement-like, crackly pattern.

Divide the dough into 500g (1lb) pieces
for small loaves, or 900g (2lb) for large.

To shape, use a plastic scraper to
scoop the dough onto a floured
surface. Lightly dust the sticky top of
the dough with rye flour and pat it into
a long rectangle. As gently as you can,
roll up the dough into a cylinder and,
using your metal scraper, place each
loaf into a butter-greased loaf tin.

Repeat with the remaining dough.

Dust the top of each loaf with plenty of
spelt flour and prove in a warm place
(25–30°C/77–86°F) for 1–2 hours until
the surface of the dough has that lovely
pavement-like pattern again.

Preheat the oven to 225°C (435°F).
Place a roasting tin on the bottom shelf
of the oven and fill with 250g (9oz) of
just-boiled water. Place the loaf tins
on the middle shelf of your oven and
bake for 45–55 minutes until nice and
dark. Check if they're done by inserting
a skewer: the loaf will have some
moistness, but there should not be a
lot of sticky dough on the skewer.

Turn out the loaves and cool on a wire
rack; try to resist eating them for 4–6
hours. This bread is incredible for a
Scandinavian lunch snack – top with
smoked salmon if you're feeling fancy,
or mayo and boiled potatoes for a
traditional Danish double-carb delight.

Horse Bread

Horse bread dates back to medieval Europe and, as the name suggests, was originally used to feed livestock. Until times of famine, that is, when the less fortunate would resort to eating this extremely bran-heavy bread themselves. The original recipe was just bran, water and enough flour to form a dough, promptly baked into a dense flat brick that would have been virtually inedible.

When intended for human consumption, the dough would be left to sour for up to 48 hours, to leaven and add flavour to the bread. I gave this a shot and I have to say, it left me feeling sorry for those who had no choice but to eat it. It might just be the densest, most filling bread ever to have passed my lips. When the only other option is starvation, I suppose flavour would be the last thing you'd consider – but, as I'm not a medieval peasant, I thought I'd modify the recipe, taking out a lot of the bran, and adding salt and a tiny bit of leaven.

The resulting bread is the heartiest of hearty loaves, one that screams for an intensely mature cheddar to be slapped on a slice (which is exactly what I did). **RS**

Makes 2–4 loaves

Equipment
*(see the detailed equipment
   section on page 83)*

Option 1
baking stone and a roasting tin

Option 2
proving basket (or a large bowl
   lined with a tea towel) and a
   Dutch oven combo cooker
   or a heavy cast-iron pot

Ingredients
500g (1lb 2oz) strong white flour
500g (1lb 2oz) water (from the
   cold tap)
100g (3½oz) wheat or rye bran
20g (¾oz) sourdough starter
   (page 76)
10g (½oz) sea salt
rice flour or fine semolina,
   for dusting

Mix all the ingredients together by hand. Leave to rest for 10–14 hours at cool room temperature (18–21°C/64–70°F) until nearly doubled in size.

Turn out the loaf onto a floured work surface. At this stage you can do one of two things:

Option 1
Put a baking stone on the middle shelf of your oven and a roasting tin on the bottom shelf, then preheat to 250°C (480°F) or as high as your oven will go. Divide the loaf into 2–4 rough rectangles without knocking the air out.

Use your metal dough scraper to transfer these smaller loaves onto a wooden peel or a baking sheet and slide them directly onto the hot baking stone in the oven.

Being very careful not to splash yourself, fill the roasting tin on the bottom shelf with 250g (9oz) of just-boiled water. This will generate steam, which will help the loaf to rise and give it a nice shiny crust. Bake for 25–35 minutes.

Option 2
Divide the dough in half. Take each half and gently bring the edges into the middle, applying enough pressure to seal the loaf. Place, seam-side down, in a proving basket dusted with rice flour or semolina and leave in warm place to prove for 30–90 minutes until almost doubled in size.

Put a Dutch oven or heavy cast-iron pot on the middle shelf of your oven, then preheat to 250°C (480°F), or as high as your oven will go.

Bake the loaf in the Dutch oven or cast-iron pot, with the lid on, for 20 minutes, them remove the lid and bake for a further 15–20 minutes until dark brown. If the loaf is colouring too quickly, turn the oven down to 230°C (445°F). While the first loaf is baking, 'retard' the second by putting it in the fridge to slow the fermentation. Bring the oven back up to temperature before baking the second loaf.

Flatbreads

In the bakery, one of the most eagerly awaited times of day is sandwich time – but, dare we say it, sometimes a couple of slices of naturally leavened bread or baguette aren't quite right. Sometimes, I crave something a little more... pliable. Less of a doorstop, more of an envelope. This flatbread recipe was born out of a summer meltdown in my kitchen at home. In a tizz, all I wanted was smoky barbecued meat in a stretchy vessel loaded with sour cream and salsa; I wanted structural integrity and an authentic corn flavour. Is that so much to ask? Like many of our favourite recipes, a happy accident resulted in something worth keeping, and this recipe will satisfy the most ambitious burrito-builders. Serve with slow-cooked brisket, guacamole, sour cream and heaps of coriander. **RS**

Makes 8–10 flatbreads

Equipment
(see the detailed equipment section on page 83)
plastic dough scraper
metal dough scraper (also called a bench knife, you can also use your plastic one)

Ingredients
100g (3½oz) fine cornmeal (preferably masa harina)
400g (14oz) plain white (all-purpose) flour
325g (11½oz) warm water (26°C/79°F)
5g (¼oz) instant dried yeast (or 10g/½oz fresh yeast)
10g (½oz) sea salt

Put all the ingredients into a bowl and mix by hand until combined.

On a clean work surface, knead the dough by pushing it away from you and folding it back on itself for about 5 minutes, or until it is very stretchy. It will likely make a sticky mess on the surface during the early stages of kneading. If this happens, use a plastic scraper to bring it all back together and continue.

Once you have a smooth elastic dough, roll it into a ball and leave to rest in a covered bowl for 45 minutes, or until almost doubled in size.

Turn out onto a floured surface and use a metal scraper to divide into 80–100g (3–3½oz) pieces.

Ball up each piece by bringing the edges into the middle and securing with your thumb. Flip so it's seam side down, then cup your hand over the ball and pull it nice and tight. Set aside to rest for 15–20 minutes.

On a floured work surface, roll out each ball to make a very thin flatbread, about 1mm (⅟₁₆in), then fry in a dry pan for 20–30 seconds each side. Lift out of the pan and set aside on a plate.

While each flatbread is cooking, roll out another to get a production line going. This is an ideal two-player game: one frying, one rolling.

Stack the flatbreads on the plate as they're cooked and keep them covered with a clean tea towel, so they steam a little to become soft and pliable.

**There are so many processes
that go into making bread:
growing, harvesting, storing,
milling, transporting, fermenting,
mixing, proving, shaping,
retarding, baking…**

Knäckebröd

In Scandinavia, baking crispbread dates back to 500AD, when they would have been hung from the ceiling or on poles. Baked only twice a year, they were often eaten stale, which gave knäckebröd something of a bad reputation, even before Ryvita came along. We happen to think they are actually pretty tasty when made with the right flour and seeds, then topped with far too much cheese. **RS**

Makes 16 large crispbreads

Ingredients

For the leaven
10g (¾oz) sourdough starter (page 76)
50g (2oz) warm water (26°C/79°F)
25g (1oz) strong white flour
25g (1oz) strong wholemeal flour

For the dough
100g (3½oz) dark rye flour
100g (3½oz) plain white (all-purpose) flour
15g (½oz) soft brown sugar
90g (3¼oz) warm water (26–30°C/79–86°F)
2g (½ teaspoon) sea salt
2g (½ teaspoon) caraway or fennel seeds
30g (1oz) rapeseed oil
sea salt flakes, for sprinkling

Start by making the leaven by following Stage 1 on page 73.

Put all the dough ingredients into a large bowl along with your leaven and mix with your hands. Once it has all come together, knead by pushing and stretching the dough away from yourself, then rolling it back on itself, for about 5 minutes.

Using your hands, roll the dough into a ball, cover with a tea towel and leave to rest for 30–45 minutes. Do not skimp on the resting time or the dough will be too tight to roll out thinly.

Preheat the oven to 200°C (400°F).

Place your dough between two sheets of baking paper the same size as a large baking tray. Squash the dough flat, then roll out to 1mm (¹⁄₁₆in) thick. Peel off the top layer of paper and cut into 5 x 10cm (2 x 4in) rectangles.

Sprinkle with sea salt flakes and prick all over with a fork – this will stop an erratic rise but also looks pleasing.

Keeping the crackers on the baking paper, slide them onto the baking tray and bake for 15–20 minutes until dark golden brown. Leave to cool before eating with cheese, smoked salmon, terrines and pickles.

Brioche

At The Snapery Bakery, we decided that, although brioche is delicious, it's not exactly ideal for burgers, which is what it's most demanded for. Brioche is too sweet and rich to be slathered with sugary sauces, a fatty patty and a slab of melty cheese. So, of course, we had to develop a bun ideal for burger use.

I have increased the butter and sugar a touch here, making it suitable for both buns and loaves. Feel free to experiment with sugar and butter. If you're adding more fat, the dough is likely to take longer to prove, as fat acts as an inhibitor of yeast – you could add a gram or two more yeast to counteract this. **RS**

Makes 14 buns or 2 large loaves

Equipment
(see the detailed equipment section on page 83)
stand mixer with a dough hook
2 baking sheets for buns, or 2 x 900g (2lb) loaf tins for loaves

Ingredients
For the leaven
75g (2½oz) strong white flour
75g (2½oz) warm water (26–30°C/79–86°F)
15g (½oz) sourdough starter (page 76)

For the dough
65g (2¼oz) whole milk
3 medium eggs
400g (14oz) strong white flour
9g (⅓oz) instant dried yeast
80g (3oz) caster (superfine) sugar
9g (⅓oz) sea salt
180g (6¼oz) butter, softened

For the egg wash
1 large egg, lightly beaten

Start by making the leaven by following Stage 1 on page 73.

The next day, to make the dough, mix the leaven with the milk and eggs in the bowl of a stand mixer fitted with a dough hook. Add the flour, yeast, sugar and salt (keeping the salt and yeast on opposite sides of the bowl, so the salt doesn't de-activate the yeast).

Mix on a slow speed until the ingredients are combined, then mix on a fast speed for a further 3–6 minutes, or until the dough starts to come away from the bowl. Let the dough rest in the bowl for 5 minutes.

With the mixer on its slowest speed, gradually add the butter, a spoonful at a time, and keep mixing until it is completely incorporated.

Roll the dough into a large ball and place it in a large bowl. Cover with a damp tea towel and leave to rest at room temperature for 45 minutes.

Remove the tea towel and, instead, cover the bowl with plastic wrap/clingfilm. Put the dough in the freezer for 1½–2 hours, then transfer to the fridge and chill overnight. This will stop it over-proving.

The next day, line two large baking sheets with parchmen paper.

Flour the top of the dough and encourage it out of the bowl onto a work surface. Roll out with a rolling pin to 1–1½cm (½–¾in), using minimal flour.

continued >>

For burger buns

Use a metal scraper (or a regular knife) to divide the dough into 70g (2½oz) squares. Take one of the squares and fold the four corners into the middle. Place seam-side down on your work surface, then cup your hand over the top, making sure your palm is touching the dough.

Using a circular anticlockwise motion, roll it into a tight ball without tearing, then place on the lined baking trays. Repeat with the rest of the dough, leaving a generous 8cm (3in) space between buns. Prove in a draught-free place at about 26°C (79°F) for 3–4 hours until the buns have just over doubled in size. One problem you may encounter is a skin forming on the buns before they have fully proved. If this happens, try using your oven as a proving chamber: with the oven off, place your trayed-up buns on the shelves, then put a bowl of hot, but not boiling, water underneath – this will create enough moisture to prevent a skin forming. Remove the buns when they are almost doubled in size and set aside.

For loaves

Grease 2 x 900g (2lb) loaf tins with butter. Either add 8–9 x 70g (2½oz) balls of dough, or 2 x 250g (9oz) balls of dough. Prove for 3½–5 hours, or until trebled in size (using the oven as your proving chamber, as described above).

When you're ready to bake, place a roasting tin at the bottom of the oven, then preheat to 180°C (350°F). If your buns or loaves look ready before the oven is up to temperature, you can transfer them to the fridge. (In fact, this can be quite a useful thing to do even if you're not waiting for the oven to heat up. When you chill your proved brioche, it firms up slightly, making it easier to egg wash.)

Egg wash your buns or loaves, load them into the oven and carefully pour just-boiled water into the roasting tin to generate steam – this will help the brioche to rise. Bake buns for 16–20 minutes until dark golden. Loaves will need 25–30 minutes – if they're looking golden after 20 minutes, turn the oven down to 160°C (320°F) and continue baking until well risen and dark golden on top. Remove from the oven and turn out on a wire rack. Then make French toast or a decadent burger.

Here is the perfect recipe for a book called Bread & Butter. Thanks, France!

Kanelbullar

We make Swedish cinnamon buns purely for the addictive joy they inject into your brain. They come with a warning: these are the narcotics of the bun world – make at your own risk. **RS**

Makes 15 buns

Equipment
*(see the detailed equipment
    section on page 83)*
stand mixer with a dough hook
2 muffin tins (optional)

Ingredients
For the dough
24g (1oz) cardamom seeds
160g (5¾oz) butter
480g (1lb 1oz) whole milk
800g (1lb 12oz) strong
    white flour
140g (5oz) caster (superfine)
    sugar
19g (¾oz) instant dried yeast
1 large egg
12g (½oz) sea salt

For the filling
280g (10oz) butter, softened
200g (7oz) dark soft brown
    sugar
8g (¼oz) ground cinnamon

For the glaze
50g (1¾oz) apricot jam
50g (1¾oz) fine-cut marmalade
25g (1oz) water

For the topping
1 large egg, lightly beaten,
    for the egg wash
pearl sugar or demerara sugar

Grind the cardamom seeds to a fine powder. You can either use a coffee/spice grinder or a pestle and mortar if you're feeling strong. (You can also use pre-ground cardamom, but it doesn't have the flavour of freshly ground.)

Put a medium saucepan on a low heat. Add the butter and ground cardamom and heat until melted. Keep on a low heat for a few more minutes to infuse, but don't let the butter brown or burn.

Weigh the milk into a large bowl, add the melted butter and cardamom and leave to cool for an hour.

Pour the cooled milk, butter and cardamom into the bowl of a stand mixer fitted with a dough hook. Add the flour, sugar, yeast, egg and salt (keeping the salt and yeast on opposite sides of the bowl, so the salt doesn't de-activate the yeast).

Mix on a slow speed until combined, then mix on a fast speed for 3–4 minutes. This is a strange dough: it will be quite sticky, but that's OK. Turn it out onto a floured work surface and gather it into a ball.

Leave to prove in a large bowl, covered with a damp tea towel, at room temperature for 30 minutes. Roll it around to make into a ball once more (it might have flattened slightly as it livens up) then let it rise for a further 15 minutes at room temperature. Replace the damp tea towel with

plastic wrap/clingfilm and put the dough in the freezer until cold all the way through (a couple of hours). You can either roll out and shape your buns now, or keep the dough in the fridge overnight and make buns the next day.

For the filling, mix the butter with the sugar and cinnamon until fully combined. Set aside.

When you're ready to shape the buns, line two baking trays with baking paper. Roll out the dough into a 60cm x 60cm (24in x 24in) square – it should be about 2–3mm ¹/₈in) thick. Spread the top two-thirds of the dough with the filling. Now fold the bottom third up and the top third down to enclose the filling completely.

Using a rolling pin, roll the filled dough away from you until it is 25cm x 60cm (10in x 24in). Cut into 15 strips approximately 2cm (¾in) thick – each strip should weigh roughly 100g (3½oz). You can roll each strip into a spiral and place in greased muffin tins, or follow the more traditional method, as follows…

Hold a strip between your thumb and middle finger so it dangles down. With your other hand, grasp the other end of the strip and bring it towards you, looping it up and over your index finger (making sure there is about a 2cm (¾in) gap between your index and middle fingers), then loop it round a second time. Start to loop the dough a third

continued >>

time, but stop one quarter of the way round as you get to your thumb. Secure with your thumb, then stretch the remaining length of dough so there is enough excess to wrap around the whole bun and gather your loops together. Plug the end of the dough into the gap created by your middle and index fingers, then gently remove your fingers – you should have a loopy knot shape – see pictures on pages 130–131. Repeat with the remaining dough strips.

Place the buns on the baking trays about 2cm (¾in) apart, then leave to prove in a warm, draught-free place (approximately 26°C/79°F) for 1½–2 hours until slightly risen.

Meanwhile, make the glaze. Heat all the ingredients in a small saucepan and simmer gently for 5–10 minutes, or until there are no lumps at all – it takes a surprising amount of time for the jam to melt properly. (If you want a perfectly smooth glaze without any lumps of fruit and shreds from the marmalade, strain it through a fine-mesh sieve.)

When you're ready to bake your buns, place a roasting tin at the bottom of the oven, then preheat to 200°C (400°F).

Egg wash the buns, then carefully pour boiling water into the roasting tin to generate steam – this will help the buns to rise. Bake for 18–22 minutes until dark golden.

Brush the glaze over the buns while they're still hot, then leave to cool for 10 minutes before sprinkling with pearl or demerara sugar.

Enjoy – and try not to overdose.

You can leave the dough in the fridge overnight and bake the buns for breakfast.

Hot Cross Buns

A favourite Easter treat. It bothers me that these buns aren't popular the rest of the year. Over Easter we gorge on them, and still can't get enough. They are delicious toasted with butter and we'll devour them at any opportunity. Why is it then that, after Easter, we put them to bed and won't even think about having another until the following year? This needs to stop! Let's eat them all year round and stop denying deliciousness! **RS**

Makes 14 buns

Equipment
(see the detailed equipment section on page 83)
stand mixer with a dough hook
piping bag fitted with a fine nozzle

Ingredients
For the leaven
40g (1½oz) strong white flour
40g (1½oz) warm water (26–30°C/79–86°F)
10g (¹⁄₃oz) sourdough starter (page 76)

For the dough
120g (4oz) sultanas (golden raisins)
250g (8¾oz) freshly brewed Earl Grey tea
65g (2¼oz) mixed candied peel
1g (¼ teaspoon) ground mixed spice
1g (¼ teaspoon) ground cinnamon
1g (¼ teaspoon) ground cardamom
finely grated zest of 1 orange
180g (6¼oz) whole milk
1 large egg
25g (1oz) butter
50g (1¾oz) caster (superfine) sugar

200g (7oz) strong white flour, extra for dusting
4g (1 teaspoon) sea salt
9g (¹⁄₃oz) instant dried yeast

For the cross paste
40g (1½oz) plain white (all-purpose) flour
35g (1¼oz) warm water
5g (¼oz) sunflower oil
1g (¼ teaspoon) salt

For the egg wash
1 large egg, lightly beaten

For the glaze
50g (1¾oz) apricot jam
1 tablespoon water
1 tablespoon rum

continued >>

**If there is not, at the
very least, a puddle
of butter – please add
a little more.**

>>

Start by making the leaven by following Stage 1 on page 73. At the same time, soak the sultanas in the hot tea to plump them up; once cooled, cover and leave in the fridge overnight.

The next day, drain the sultanas and transfer to a large bowl, then add the mixed peel, spices and orange zest. Combine well and set aside.

Next, make the dough. Put the leaven, milk, egg, butter, sugar, flour, salt and yeast into the bowl of a stand mixer fitted with a dough hook (keep the salt and yeast on opposite sides of the bowl, so the salt doesn't de-activate the yeast).

Mix on a slow speed until combined, with no dry clumps of flour visible, then mix on a fast speed for 3–5 minutes until the dough is coming away from the sides of the bowl and is looking strong and elastic. Leave the dough to rest in the mixer for 5 minutes.

Add the dried fruit and spice mixture and mix on a slow speed until fully incorporated.

Turn out the dough onto a floured work surface and shape into a ball, then transfer to a large bowl and cover with a damp tea towel. Leave to prove for 45 minutes at room temperature.

Knock back the dough and shape it into a ball again, then leave to prove for a further 30 minutes until almost doubled in size.

Meanwhile, line two baking trays with baking paper.

When ready, turn out the dough onto a floured surface and flatten. Then, using a rolling pin, roll out a 1½cm (¾in) thick square.

Divide the dough into 75g (2½oz) squares and shape into balls by following the Burger Buns method on page 124.

Then place on the lined baking trays. If you want your hot cross buns to 'batch' (join together in the oven), space them close together, about 2cm (¾in) apart. If you want perfectly round, individual buns, space them about 6cm (2½in) apart. Leave to prove in a warm draught-free place (23–25°C/73–77°F) for 1½–3 hours until doubled in size.

When you're ready to bake, preheat the oven to 200°C (400°F).

Meanwhile, make the cross paste by mixing all the ingredients together until smooth. Scoop into a piping bag fitted with a fine nozzle.

Egg wash your buns, then pipe with criss-cross strips of paste, and bake in the hot oven for 16–20 minutes until dark golden.

While the buns are baking, make the glaze. Put the jam and water in a small saucepan over a medium heat and simmer for 5 minutes. Take off the heat, add the rum and stir to form a brushable syrup, you can always add more water if it's too thick.

Brush the glaze over the buns while they're still hot, so that they become enticingly sticky. Try to let them cool for an hour before eating. But, odds are, there'll be one missing before the hour is up – only a robot could resist these. Serve toasted, with plenty of butter. Bliss.

BUTTER

Cultured Butter & Buttermilk

Grant's signature butter

While working at Fäviken in Sweden, I got to know butter very well. Often the first job a chef is given is the simplest, so they can observe how the kitchen and the team operate. Mine was portioning the butter for service – so I got to taste the incredible butter on day one.

The first thing I noticed is the insanely yellow colour of the large rectangular slab inside its parchment wrapping. The second thing I noticed is the intense buttery smell – the fermented cream before churning adds a distinct butyric tang. When I broke chunks off the cold block of butter with a fork, tiny remnants would remained on the chopping board; tasting these shards made me realise just how uncared for and plain such an important staple ingredient had come to be, and it made me want everyone in the world to taste something as good as this.

I constantly experiment to reach the best butter recipe for the current butter I produce and I encourage you to do the same at home. The best variable to experiment with is the starter culture – this is the bacteria that ferments the cream before churning. More about this on pages 146–149.

To pick your starter culture, start by choosing your favourite sour cream or crème fraîche, or even a thick, set yogurt (ensuring it isn't the low-fat variety). The flavour you taste in this is the lactic bacteria, and it is this lactobacillus that will culture the cream that you will churn to become your butter – in other words, the flavour of that lactic bacteria will be reflected in the finished butter.

Next, you need to find a really good-quality double cream, with approximately 40% fat. You'll need twice the amount of cream than the amount of butter you want to make –

I recommend starting with 1 litre (1 quart), which will give you a 500g (1lb 2oz) pat of butter. And if you want to adapt the quantities in the recipe, stick to a ratio of 10% starter to cream.

I source cream from select Jersey and Guernsey herds at specific farms, but most farmers' markets will have a supplier of great dairy products.

Pasteurisation means we're used to blander dairy products. While the process renders the products safe, it doesn't distinguish between good and bad bacteria, but removes them all, including harmless ones that bring unique flavours to dairy products.

Despite my great love for raw milk and its beautiful flavours, I ironically use pasteurised cream to make my butter. While raw milk has a natural and beautiful microflora showcasing all the wonderful bacterial flavours present in milk, I aim to produce one specific-flavour butter, and pasteurised cream is a beautiful 'blank canvas' that allows me to do this.

I still continue to look for the bacteria that produces the best 'butter' flavours and I buy many freeze-dried individual strains of lactobacillus to test with, but the following recipe reflects my first experience of exploring the flavour of butter by fermenting creams with bacteria I could find readily available. **GH**

continued >>

Spread your butter so thickly that you might mistake it for cheese

**Makes about 500g (1lb 2oz)
butter and an equal amount
cultured buttermilk**

Equipment
large mixing bowl
piece of muslin (cheesecloth)
    large enough to cover the
    mixing bowl
electric stand mixer or hand-
    held electric beaters
digital thermometer
cold, clean surface

Ingredients
1 litre (1 quart) 40% fat high-
    quality double (thick) cream
100ml (3½fl oz) sour cream,
    crème fraîche or yogurt,
    which is the starter
rock salt, to taste (approx.
    20g/¾oz)

In a large and spotlessly clean bowl, mix together your cream and starter (sour cream, crème fraîche or yogurt), stirring well to make sure the starter is fully incorporated.

Cover the bowl with muslin and leave at room temperature (about 25°C/77°F) for 20 hours.

When the time is up replace the muslin with plastic wrap/clingfilm and chill in the fridge for a further 20 hours.

Remove the cultured cream from the fridge and leave it at room temperature for about an hour, or until it has warmed to around 8–14°C (46–57°F). This chilling and warming encourages the bacteria to develop and the cream to ferment.

Now we're ready to churn. Using an electric stand mixer or hand-held beaters on medium-high speed (or even whisking by hand if you've got arms like an ox) begin to whisk your cultured cream. It's important to have your bowl no more than half full, as the cream will expand before it splits.

When the cream completely splits to form yellow globules (called popcorn butter) and liquid (buttermilk), strain through a sieve, reserving both the popcorn butter and the buttermilk. This cultured buttermilk will keep for 12 days in the fridge.

Quickly knead the popcorn butter on a cold, clean surface by working it with the heels of your hands, squeezing out any remaining buttermilk until all the moisture has been removed from your butter.

Season with salt to taste. Then hand-knead the butter again to release any final excess of moisture.

The cultured butter will keep for up to 3 weeks in the fridge, and will continue to mature and develop over that time.

The science of butter

For a product made predominantly from one ingredient (cream), butter has a surprisingly interesting story. To really understand it, it's helpful to delve into the physics – or at least touch on it – as well as run through the process of making butter.

First there's the milk, ideally from a well-bred Jersey cow. I use Jersey and Guernsey herd milk, due to the breeds' ability to produce an extremely high-fat and beta-carotene-rich milk. Beta carotene is naturally present in grass and it is what gives milk its fat-rich yellow pigment. The more grass a cow eats, the yellower the milk will appear – that's why summer cheeses and butters are much more colourful than those made in winter. For me, butter should be yellow, so choosing a cow's milk that has the capacity to produce a beautiful yellow butter has always been a priority.

Milk is a liquid with butterfat naturally emulsified within in it. The fat cells have a lower density to water, which is why we see cream rise to the top of a milk bottle – at least the unhomogenised milk the milkman used to deliver in glass bottles. (A favourite childhood story from my mum is the race between her and her brother to the front door to see who could get the cream from the milk on to their cornflakes.)

Separating the cream from the rest of the milk is the next part of the process. Historically (before industrialisation), fresh milk would be left out in a large vat. After a day or two the cream will have naturally risen to the top of the vat and would then be skimmed (ladled) off from the top, leaving 'skimmed' milk left over.

Once centrifuges (a machine that spins at such a velocity that the cream rises higher than the milk) were introduced, the traditional techniques became obsolete.

You can make butter from fresh cream, but to make cultured butter (which has vastly more flavour), you need to ferment the cream. In Scandinavia, the very traditional technique would be to collect the cream (skimmed from the daily milk that was milked from the cows throughout summer) in wooden vessels. By constantly reusing these vessels, a dominant lactobacillus held in the grain of the wood that allowed the cultures in the cream to thrive and multiply, thereby fermenting the cream. Essentially, this is a process of lactic bacteria feeding off the lactose in the cream to produce lactic acid, which gives the cream a specific taste and acidity.

Home butter-makers today can mimic this process by adding a cultured dairy product to the cream, such as sour cream or crème fraîche – this is the starter for the butter. Bacteria has the ability to produce a pretty much infinite range and combination of flavours, so it's worth experimenting with your favourites.

You can buy freeze-dried cultures online to make butter, but it's more important to experiment with sour cream or crème fraîche as your starter to really experience the potential flavour possibilities.

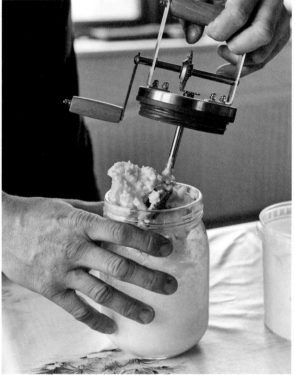

Small paddle churns were a common feature in households from the nineteenth century onwards, but to be honest, shaking a normal jam jar is just as good.

For this newly fermented cream to become butter, it must be agitated. Agitating the fat globules that are emulsified within a liquid means that the membranes of the fat molecule (made of proteins and phospholipids) begin to break down, and the fat slowly begins to bond within the agitating liquid.

As the agitation progresses and fat globules begin to form, they group with more and more globules and can finally be seen visibly.

The liquid proteins released by splitting the emulsion is named 'buttermilk' and the visible globules of butter is known among butter-makers as 'butter popcorn' (my favourite time to taste).

There's a beautiful and historic selection of techniques used to agitate butter that range from wooden plungers that forced the cream to move to spinning beaters that applied even more agitation force. Then barrel churns (where the barrel is rotated allowing the cream to be in much a tumble dryer style motion) took over.

It's great fun (especially for children) to explore the physics of this and it's very easy to replicate at home using a jam jar. Cream can be placed in a jar or sealable vessel, it's important to only half fill the container as air space is very important for the motion to function properly. Then the jar needs to be vigorously shaken, making sure that as the cream thickens it falls away from the sides of the vessel. As long as there's agitation and the temperature doesn't rise over room temperature, it should work. I put this to the test once by half-filling a bottle with cream and hanging it off the back of a

sailing boat: the constant motion of the waves hitting the bottle made us delicious butter within 45 minutes.

Once you have separated the buttermilk from the butter popcorn, it's time to create the finished product. Cold hands are actually one of the most important elements from here on out as you need to hand knead the mixture to release the buttermilk. Buttermilk has such a delicious flavour and acidity you don't want to wash it all out, but it's also high in proteins which bacteria love, so if you leave in too much buttermilk, the butter could over produce bacteria and end up tasting overly sour and cheesy.

The butter needs to be hand kneaded until it no longer looks wet and only a few cold squeezes releases a few drops of buttermilk. For me, this is the perfect stage to stop and finally add salt, also by hand. The salt further draws moisture, so once the salt has drawn excess moisture, butter should be kneaded again to release any final excess of moisture.

And there you have it: with the noble help of physics, you can create the yellow gold that we consider a staple ingredient.

Cultured Butter Variations

My whole motivation for making butter is to make it more, well, buttery, and certain ingredients really complement milk fat: think rich flavours – herbal, smoky, salty and verdant. The following are my all-time-favourite things to add to a great butter. **GH**

Wild Garlic Butter

When in season between March and June, wild garlic is easy to find in most Northern European woodlands, and it offers an abundance of pungent deliciousness. This butter is my favourite way of preserving the fresh garlic flavour. Once blended and rolled into a log, it can be easily frozen for use throughout the year. Outstandingly simple and satisfying stirred through hot pasta.

Makes about 200g (7oz)

Ingredients
60g (2oz) wild garlic leaves (ramsons), finely chopped
200g (7oz) Cultured Butter (page 140), softened

Fold the wild garlic into the butter.

Place on a piece of plastic wrap/clingfilm and roll into a log, then twist and tie the ends to seal. Freeze until needed. The butter will keep for up to 3 weeks in the fridge, and will continue to mature and develop over that time.

Seaweed Butter

Seaweed types vary, this recipe works well with pepper dulse, which can be foraged in the UK and dried at home. However, a high quality nori from a Japanese food supplier can be just as rich and savoury. This is an incredible finishing butter atop fresh fish – try it with steamed haddock and you'll be sold.

Makes about 200g (7oz)

Ingredients
30g (1oz) finely chopped dried seaweed
200g (7oz) Cultured Butter (page 140), softened

Fold the seaweed into room temperature butter using the back of a spoon.

Place on a piece of plastic wrap/clingfilm and roll into a log, then twist and tie the ends to seal. Freeze until needed. The butter will keep for up to 3 weeks in the fridge, and will continue to mature and develop over that time.

From top: Bone Marrow Butter; Wild Garlic Butter; Seaweed Butter; Smoked Butter; Sundried Tomato Butter

Bone Marrow Butter

The best thing to add to butter is another deliciously rich and fatty ingredient derived from a cow. Sliced and left to melt on top of a large roasted joint of meat, an individual steak or whole roast portobello mushrooms, this butter is incredible.

Makes about 200g (7oz)

Ingredients
2 or 3 sections of marrow bone (from your butcher)
150g (5½oz) Cultured Butter (page 140), softened
2 banana shallots, finely chopped
20g (¾oz) Parmesan, finely grated
small handful of finely chopped flat-leaf parsley
sea salt flakes and cracked black pepper

Preheat the oven to 180°C (350°F).

Put the bones into a roasting tin and roast for 20 minutes until the marrow is meltingly soft. When the bones are cool enough to handle, scrape out the marrow into a bowl.

Heat a small knob of the butter in a frying pan over a medium-low heat, then gently cook the shallots with a pinch of salt until they are very soft but not coloured, about 10 minutes. Set aside to cool.

Add the remaining butter to the bowl of bone marrow, then fold in the cooled shallots, Parmesan and parsley. Season with salt and pepper to taste.

Place the butter on a piece of plastic wrap/clingfilm and roll into a log, then twist and tie the ends to seal. Keep in the fridge for up to 3 days, ready for steak night, or freeze until needed.

Smoked Butter

As soon as I started making butter I had requests from everyone to make a smoked butter. From hot-smoking ghee to cold-smoking blocks of cultured butter, this soon became an entertaining pastime in the turbulent life of a butter maker. Smoked ghee was beautiful, but I couldn't really call it butter – it's just not solid enough! And cold-smoked freshly churned butter had a harsh smokiness to it that threatened to overwhelm the flavour of the butter. In the end, the best results came as a complete surprise, by way of some mailed samples of oak-smoked sea salt from my preferred UK salt supplier, Halen Môn, based in Anglesey. As well as being incredibly easy to make, this cultured butter is given the perfect flavour boost by the salt's subtle smoky notes.

Makes about 500g (1lb 2oz)

Ingredients
500g (1lb 2oz) unsalted Cultured
   Butter (page 140), softened
15g (½oz) oak-smoked sea salt

When you follow the method for Cultured Butter on page 140, replace the salt with oak-smoked sea salt at the last step.

Place on a piece of plastic wrap/clingfilm and roll into a log, then twist and tie the ends to seal. Leave to rest in the fridge for 2 days, to give the smoke flavours time to permeate throughout the butter, then freeze until needed or decadently melt over chargrilled scallops. Delicious.

Sundried Tomato Butter

Sundried tomatoes are super rich and meaty, I would normally use this whole serving of butter to finish the perfect tomato risotto.

Makes about 200g (7oz)

Ingredients
50g (1¾) sundried tomatoes,
   very finely chopped
200g (7oz) Cultured Butter
   (page 140), softened

Fold the sundried tomatoes into the room temperature butter using the back of a spoon.

Place on a piece of plastic wrap/clingfilm and roll into a log, then twist and tie the ends to seal. Freeze until needed. The butter will keep for up to 3 weeks in the fridge, and will continue to mature and develop over that time.

Cultured Crème Fraîche & Sour Cream

Taking good care of the milk is vital when making dairy products, and the same applies to cream when it comes to making butter. Traditionally, culturing cream was primarily a way of prolonging its life. Before the dairy industry was revolutionised by electronic cream separators and pasteurisation, milk would be left outside in large vats to naturally separate. After one day, the cream would rise to the top and its cultures would be start to develop.

I wanted to create a recipe that harked back to this era, while also nodding to my time in Scandinavia – where sour cream seems to be served with everything. I hope the following shows my appreciation of cultured cream, as well as the ingredients that can really enhance its flavour and align it to the four seasons: burnt hay for the harvest in late summer; bottarga for the taste of autumn; horseradish, which is unearthed in the winter; and lastly fresh garlic, for the bountiful spring. **GH**

Toasted Hay Cream

I'm aware that this recipe may raise some eyebrows (but hopefully not singe any!). You'll want to find food-safe hay, in other words, one that has not been sprayed with pesticides. If you don't have a trusty farmer to hand, your best bet is to head to a pet shop, where organic hay is more common than in garden centres. The toasty earthiness of the hay complements very sweet desserts, particularly when churned into ice cream. Alternatively, smother on light crackers with a drizzle of olive oil and a sprinkle of sesame seeds.

Makes 550ml (19fl oz)

Ingredients
100g (3½oz) hay
500ml (17fl oz) raw double
   (thick) cream
50ml (2fl oz) Cultured Buttermilk
   (page 140)

Put the hay in a ceramic or terracotta pot and carefully set it alight, then let it burn down to ash. Take a heaped teaspoon of the hay ash and pass it through a fine sieve.

Place the sieved hay ash in a food processor, add the cream and buttermilk and blitz to combine.

Transfer the cream mixture to a spotlessly clean bowl and then culture the cream by following steps in paragraphs 2–4 of the Cultured Butter recipe on page 144.

Once the cream is cultured, refrigerate for up to a week.

Bottarga Cream

This is great served on Nordic Fjellbrød (page 108) with smoked salmon and dill. Or replace the bottarga with an equal amount of English autumn or Australian winter truffle, which taste amazing with ground meat pierogi tossed in bacon fat.

Makes 220ml (7¾fl oz)

Ingredients
200ml (7fl oz) raw double (thick) cream
20ml (¾fl oz) Cultured Buttermilk (page 140)
40g (1½oz) bottarga, finely grated
sea salt (optional)

Put the cream into a spotlessly clean bowl and thoroughly mix in the buttermilk, then culture the cream by following the steps in paragraphs 2–4 of the Cultured Butter recipe on page 144.

Fold the bottarga into the cultured cream and taste for seasoning, adding a little salt if necessary – the bottarga usually provides enough seasoning by itself. Use within 1 week.

Horseradish Cream

For meat-eaters, this is a joy served alongside beef, mackerel or oysters. For vegetarians, serve with beetroot, fermented green tomatoes or peas.

Makes 250ml (8¾fl oz)

Ingredients
200ml (7fl oz) raw double (thick) cream
20ml (¾fl oz) Cultured Buttermilk (page 140)
50g (1¾oz) fresh horseradish root, washed, peeled and grated
large pinch of sea salt

Put the cream into a spotlessly clean bowl and thoroughly mix in the buttermilk, then culture the cream by following the steps in paragraphs 2–4 of the Cultured Butter recipe on page 144.

Fold the horseradish into the cultured cream, adding salt to taste. Transfer to an airtight container and refrigerate for a minimum of 24 hours, or up to a week, to allow the flavour to develop – the longer it is kept, the hotter it will be. But do use it up within 1 week.

Garlic Cream

This should keep in the fridge for 3 days, and makes a great base for pasta sauces and salad dressings.

Makes 220ml (7¾fl oz)

Ingredients
200ml (7fl oz) raw double (thick) cream
20ml (¾fl oz) Cultured Buttermilk (page 140)
1 garlic clove, finely grated
large pinch of sea salt

Put the cream into a spotlessly clean bowl and thoroughly mix in the buttermilk, then culture the cream by following the steps in paragraphs 2–4 of the Cultured Butter recipe on page 144.

Fold the garlic and salt into the cultured cream, then taste for seasoning and adjust as needed. Use within 3 days.

From top: Bottarga cream; Garlic Cream; Horseradish Cream

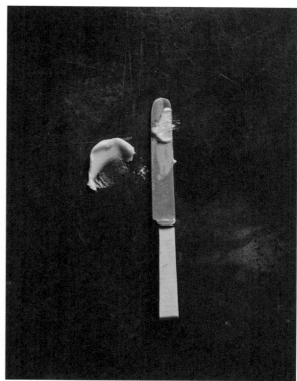

Farmers will put their cows in the field in spring: as the cows eat more green vegetation, the summer butters will have a rich, grassy flavour.

Butter Braised Vegetables

This is inspired by two food writers I greatly admire, Jennifer McLagan and Molly Wizenburg – reading their recipes always makes me feel as if I am right next to them in their kitchens. Neither of these accomplished cooks ever shies away from flavour, and they clearly have a wholehearted understanding of slow-cooked, comforting dishes such as this one.

In her blog, Orangette, Molly includes one of Jennifer's recipes, which she describes as endive swimming in a 'brothy sauce of their own juices, enriched and mellowed with butter, brightened with citrus'. And this led me to look beyond endive to other vegetables that would benefit from a buttery bath. **EH**

Serves 4 as a side dish

Ingredients
200g (7oz) Cultured Butter
    (page 140)
4 Jerusalem artichokes
1 fennel bulb
2 heads of endive (chicory)
2 leeks
4 spring onions (scallions)
juice of 1 lemon
sea salt and freshly ground
    black pepper
crusty bread and crumbly
    cheese, to serve

Preheat the oven to 160ºC (320ºF).

Put the butter into a large roasting tin and place in the oven on the middle shelf so that it melts and starts to foam.

Meanwhile, prepare the vegetables. Halve the Jerusalem artichokes, fennel and endive. Cut two slits crossways down the length of the leeks, starting halfway up the white part (leaving them intact at the base) and continuing to the end of the green part, so the leeks fan out easily. Trim the spring onions but keep them whole.

Add the artichokes and fennel to the hot roasting tin, thoroughly coating them in the browning butter. Season with salt and pepper and cook for 45 minutes.

Then add the leeks, endive and spring onions to the roasting tin, basting and seasoning well. Return everything to the oven for another 45 minutes, or until all the vegetables are golden, soft and delectable.

Squeeze over the lemon juice, then serve with crusty bread and perhaps a little crumbly cheese.

Butter Poached Turbot

Poaching fish in butter is a very delicate and rewarding technique that can be used for almost any whole fish. A large whole fish such as turbot is a perfect showstopper for a dinner party, but a smaller fish, such as brown trout, makes for an easy, more intimate supper. Once it is completely submerged in the cooking liquor, the fish is cooked by a very gentle heat, which preserves all its flavour and texture. The skin can be pulled off in one piece and the flesh should come away from the bones easily, ready to be devoured. **GH**

Serves 6

Equipment
digital thermometer

Ingredients
1 x 1½kg (3lb 5oz) whole turbot, cleaned and gutted (Dover sole, plaice or brill would also work well)
30g (1oz) rock salt
200ml (7fl oz) apple cider vinegar
1kg (2lb 4oz) Cultured Butter (page 140)
sea salt and freshly ground black pepper
fresh bread and a green salad, to serve

Cover the fish with 20g (¾oz) of the rock salt and set aside at room temperature for at least 2 hours prior to cooking to draw out any excess moisture. Preheat the oven to 100°C (212°F).

Half-fill the sink with cold water and put a large saucepan on a medium heat. Add the remaining salt, the vinegar and butter to the pan and bring to a light simmer.

Carefully place the pan in the sink of cold water and cool the butter mixture until it reads 65°C (150°F) on a digital thermometer. Whisk thoroughly, then transfer half the butter mixture to a roasting tin large enough to hold the whole fish.

Using the flat edge of a knife against the skin, skim the salt and excess moisture from the fish and use kitchen paper to pat dry. Immerse the fish in the buttery poaching liquor, skin-side up, then pour the remaining butter mixture over the top of the fish. Slide the tin into the oven and cook for about 1 hour. It's hard to be exact as larger fish may need as long as 1½ hours. For smaller fish, aim for 10 minutes for every 1cm (½in) thickness of the fish. When cooked, the flesh should appear opaque, clean and white but slightly translucent in the very centre.

The cooked fish will be quite delicate, so use a large fish slice and extra care to lift it onto a serving plate and season. Take the fish to the table whole, for people to help themselves, alongside fresh bread and a crisp green salad.

Sieve and cool the leftover poaching liquor – it can be reused at least once to poach fish again. It should last no more than 2 days in the fridge but can be frozen for up to 6 months.

Butter Steak

This is the quickest recipe in the book, and although some of the lengthier recipes require patience and time to create their flavoursome punch, the intense flavour of this one is not diminished by its speediness. A decadent dish to satisfy your greedy, impulsive side. **EH**

<u>**Serves 1**</u>

Equipment
digital thermometer

Ingredients
1 x 250g (9oz) rib-eye steak
2 tablespoons rapeseed oil
 (or other oil that can withstand
 high temperatures)
2 garlic cloves, bruised
2 sprigs rosemary
small handful of thyme
small handful of flat-leaf parsley
50g (1¾oz) Cultured Butter
 (page 140)
sea salt and freshly ground
 black pepper
sourdough bread and a
 dressed green salad,
 to serve

Take the steak out of the fridge an hour before you want to cook it, to let it come to room temperature.

When you're ready to begin cooking, put a medium frying pan over a high heat until it is piping hot. Test by flicking a little water onto the pan – it should spit back at you and immediately evaporate. Add the oil and swirl it around so it coats the bottom of the pan nicely.

Season the steak, then carefully place in the pan and fry for 2 minutes.

Turn the steak and continue to cook until it's done to your liking. To test if it's done you can press a digital thermometer to its centre (50°C/122°F for rare, 60°C/140°F for medium rare, 65°C/149°F for medium). Alternatively, make a fist and press the soft fleshy part of your hand, between your thumb and your forefinger, then press the steak: a rare steak should feel like a loose fist, a medium-rare steak like a slightly clenched fist, and a medium-well done steak like a tightly clenched fist. Remember to cook the steak slightly under how you want it, as it will continue to cook during its resting time.

As soon as your steak is ready, remove the pan from the heat, place the garlic and herbs underneath the steak and place the butter and more seasoning on top of the steak.

Let it rest for a minute while you dress the salad and slice some bread.

Spoon the melted butter over the steak, or use the herbs to brush the buttery juices over it. The heat from the steak should have released the essential oils from the rosemary and thyme to give a beautiful aroma. Discard the herbs, transfer the steak to a plate, and pour any remaining pan juices over the top. Eat immediately and mop up the juices with sourdough.

Butter Sauces

Butter makes a sauce complete, and a sauce can complete a dish. Whether it's the nutty, light flavours of a beurre noisette, which somehow complement any pan-fried fish, or a béarnaise served atop a perfectly cooked cut of sirloin, sauces can transform a meal. Think of elevating your steak dinner with rounded, buttery, verdant notes (it's almost like returning the cow to its field!). Or using the classic French beurre blanc, which will happily accompany any poached meat, fish or vegetable – from John Dory to home-grown carrots – with its grassy chives, and a rich butteriness offset by the wine's acidity. These sauces really are heaven. **GH**

Beurre Noisette

Makes about 200ml (7fl oz)

Ingredients
200g (7oz) Cultured Butter
  (page 140)
juice of 1 lemon
sea salt and freshly ground
  black pepper

Put a frying pan over a medium-high heat.

Add the butter and heat until it turns a nut-brown colour and the milk solids (white flecks) have turned brown.

Add the lemon juice, a pinch each of salt and pepper, then remove from the heat, whisk and pour over your chosen dinner.

Beurre Blanc

Makes about 150ml (5fl oz)

Ingredients
2 banana shallots, finely
  chopped
75ml (2½fl oz) white wine
  vinegar
60ml (2fl oz) dry white wine
125g (4½oz) Cultured Butter
  (page 140), cubed
splash of extra virgin olive oil
sea salt and freshly ground
  black pepper
small bunch chives, chopped

Put the shallots, vinegar, wine and 50ml (2fl oz) water into a saucepan. Set over a medium heat and cook until only a little liquid remains.

Turn the heat down as low as it will go and whisk in the butter, one piece at a time, allowing each one to melt and emulsify before adding the next. Take the pan off the heat occasionally, to ensure the sauce doesn't overheat and split.

Once all the butter has been used, the sauce should be pale and have a thin, custard-like consistency.

Finish with the olive oil, seasoning and chives.

Hollandaise

Makes about 300ml (10fl oz)

Ingredients
300g (10½oz) Cultured Butter
    (page 140)
4 tablespoons white wine
    vinegar
4 large eggs, separated
juice of 1 lemon
sea salt flakes and freshly
    ground black pepper

For me, hollandaise is essentially a thick, warm, butter sauce, and béarnaise is its enhanced big brother. To make it, follow the method for béarnaise below, but omit the shallots and tarragon.

Béarnaise Sauce

Makes about 300ml (10fl oz)

Ingredients
300g (10½oz) Cultured Butter
    (page 140)
4 tablespoons white wine
    vinegar
4 banana shallots, finely
    chopped
3 tablespoons chopped
    tarragon
4 large eggs, separated
juice of 1 lemon
sea salt and freshly ground
    black pepper

Melt the butter in a small, heavy-based saucepan over a low heat. When the butter is foaming, remove the pan from the heat and leave it to stand for a few minutes so that the white milk solids sink to the bottom of the pan. Pour the butter through a fine sieve and discard the solids.

Put the vinegar into a medium saucepan, then add the shallots, half of the chopped tarragon and salt to taste. Let it simmer over a medium heat until the volume of liquid has reduced by more than half. Strain and leave to cool.

Lightly beat the egg yolks, then stir them into the cooled vinegar, followed by the lemon juice. Pour the mixture into a heatproof bowl set over a pan of simmering water (do not allow the base of the bowl to touch the water). Whisk constantly until the sauce has thickened enough to coat the back of a spoon and has increased slightly in volume.

Remove the bowl from the heat and pour in the clarified butter in a slow, steady stream, whisking continuously, so the mixture emulsifies to become smooth and thick. Fold in the rest of the tarragon and season to taste with salt and pepper.

Moroccan Fermented Butter

Smen (also called semneh, simin, semn or sman) is a salted fermented butter that's a prized ingredient in North African and Middle Eastern cuisine. Typically produced from goat's or sheep's milk, it smells very cheesy. My favourite item of smen trivia comes from southern Morocco where it is traditional, on the birth of a daughter, for Berber farmers to begin a ferment of smen that will be preserved and eaten on the day the daughter is wed, usually melted and tossed into hot couscous. Otherwise, smen can be used to roast and fry all sorts of delights: eggs and mushrooms work very well, as do onions and garlic when preparing the base for tagines couscous. **GH**

Makes about 500g (1lb 2oz)

Equipment
muslin (cheesecloth)
kitchen/butcher's string

Ingredients
several large sprigs thyme
   and oregano
500g (1lb 2oz) unsalted Cultured
   Butter (page 140)
1 tablespoon finely ground
   rock salt

Make a bouquet garni with the thyme and oregano by gently wrapping the herbs in a piece of muslin and tying tightly with string.

Put the butter into a large saucepan over a medium heat. Let it melt and come to a light simmer.

Add the bouquet garni and simmer for 40 minutes, or until the milk solids (white flecks) have turned golden.

Pass the butter through a muslin-lined sieve to remove the milk solids.

Stir the salt into the clarified butter and pour into a sterilised jar.

Place in a cool, dark cupboard for a minimum of 1 month. Once opened, keep refrigerated – it will last indefinitely.

Butter
Chicken Curry

It turns out hand strength is a real aid when it comes to both Brazilian jiu-jitsu and butter making, something I realised after hand-kneading two tonnes of butter in a year – and training in jiu-jitsu. Deevya, a lady in class, shared this family recipe. **GH**

Serves 4

Ingredients
500g (1lb 2oz) boneless chicken (breast fillet), cut into bite-sized pieces
200g (7oz) good butter, plus 1 tablespoon extra
1 large onion, finely chopped
2 teaspoons ground coriander
2 teaspoons ground cumin
½ teaspoon ground cardamom
½ teaspoon garam masala
1 teaspoon very finely chopped ginger
1 teaspoon very finely chopped garlic
1 x 400g (14oz) can of chopped tomatoes
1 teaspoon sea salt
¼ teaspoon dried fenugreek leaves, gently crushed
4 green chillies, finely chopped
steamed rice and naan bread, to serve

For the marinade
2 tablespoons tandoori masala spices
1 tablespoon very finely chopped ginger
1 tablespoon very finely chopped garlic
125ml (4fl oz) plain yogurt (or Cultured Buttermilk, page 140)
1 tablespoon ghee

First, marinate the chicken. Place all the marinade ingredients in a large bowl along with the chicken, mix well, then cover and leave in the fridge for at least 4 hours, preferably overnight.

When you're ready to make the curry, heat the butter in a large heavy-based pan and fry the onions over a medium heat until soft.

Add all the spices and stir well, allowing them to fry for a few minutes.

Add the ginger, garlic, tomatoes and salt, and cook for 20 minutes over a medium-low heat, then blend to a purée.

Add the chicken with its marinade to the pan and cook for 16 minutes over a medium heat, stirring often. Add the extra tablespoon of butter and the fenugreek leaves and simmer for a final 10 minutes.

Garnish with the green chillies, and serve with steamed rice and buttered naan.

Ghee

Ghee is the reason why, historically, India's butter consumption has surpassed every other country in the world! Ghee is a type of clarified butter whose butter solids have caramelised to give it a nuttier, richer taste than other clarified butters. It is traditionally used in many Indian dishes, and for healing in Ayurvedic medicine. We'd recommend it as the base for most curries, and for rice dishes such as biryani. **GH**

Makes about 200g (7oz)

Equipment
muslin (cheesecloth)

Ingredients
200g (7oz) Cultured Butter
(page 140)

Simmer the butter in a large saucepan over a low-medium heat until the milk solids (white flecks) separate out. Skim these solids from the surface with a shallow spoon and keep cooking the butter gently for 20 minutes.

Pass the clarified butter through a muslin-lined sieve to remove any impurities, then pour into a sterilised bottle or jar and store in a cool, dark place for up to 12 months.

Toasted Butter Danish Daal

Denmark may not be the most obvious place to associate with a good daal, and there is no claim of authenticity here. The idea with this recipe is to gradually build up layers of flavour, starting with the earthy alliums and spices, then acidity from the tomatoes, followed by the creaminess and richness of coconut and butter. Finally, a hit of freshness from the citrus and coriander lifts and balances the dish.

This recipe comes from a very good friend, Rebecca, who cooked this soupy daal when we lived together in Denmark. The apartment was so small my bedroom was also the kitchen – the joke that 'I spend so much time in the kitchen I might as well live there' sometimes felt rather too close to reality! With nothing but a shelf of cookbooks separating the living space from my sleeping space, it's a miracle we didn't get sick of each other. This recipe is included as a reminder of much commensality around that dining table and is a tribute to Rebecca's warmth, patience and kindness during those happy years. **EH**

>>

Serves 4

Ingredients
100g (3½oz) Cultured Butter
  (page 140)
2 small onions, finely chopped
2 small leeks, cut into thin,
  thumb-length strips
3 celery sticks, finely diced
1 cooking apple, peeled and
  finely diced
1 teaspoon ground turmeric
1 teaspoon ground cumin
1 teaspoon hot curry powder
1 tablespoon garam masala
1 x 400g (14oz) can of chopped
  tomatoes
1½ litres (1½ quarts) good
  chicken stock
75g (2½oz) split red lentils
5–6 curry leaves (or 2 bay
  leaves)
2 Kaffir lime leaves
4 green cardamom pods, seeds
  removed and reserved
2 cloves
1 cinnamon stick
finely grated zest of 1 lemon
4 garlic cloves, thinly sliced
½ teaspoon chilli flakes
1 x 400g (14oz) can of
  coconut milk
juice of 1 lime
sea salt
plenty of roughly chopped
  coriander (cilantro), to garnish
steamed rice or chapatis, roti or
  naan bread, to serve

In a large saucepan, heat half of the butter over a medium heat. After a few minutes, add the onions and leeks and cook for 10–15 minutes until golden and starting to crisp at the edges. Add the celery and apple, stir well and cook for another minute or so.

Add the turmeric, cumin, curry powder, garam masala and 1 teaspoon of salt. Carefully cook the spices for 5 minutes to release all their beautiful aromas, stirring them often so they don't burn.

Add the tomatoes and simmer for 5 minutes.

Stir in the stock, lentils, curry leaves, Kaffir lime leaves, cardamom seeds, cloves, cinnamon stick and lemon zest. Simmer on a low heat for 30 minutes, skimming away any foam that rises to the surface with a large spoon.

When the daal is almost done, heat the remaining butter in a small frying pan over a low heat and gently fry the garlic until it is a very pale gold, taking care not to let it colour too much.

When the lentils are cooked and the daal has thickened add the chilli flakes, coconut milk and half of the lime juice and simmer for 5 minutes.

Check the seasoning and add more salt if needed, then stir through the remaining lime juice. Top with the sliced garlic and toasted butter and garnish with chopped coriander. The daal is beautiful by itself, but can also be served with steamed rice and Indian breads.

Tibetan Butter Tea

This tea, known as *po cha*, is definitely an acquired taste, but I'd recommend it for the hardiest of butter lovers.

In Tibet, cultured yak butter is commonly eaten, and a traditional butter churn called a *mdong mo* is used to prepare the tea; it is considered that the longer the tea is churned, the better it tastes. Sometimes rancid butter is used to give a different, sought-after taste – but this option might be best suited to mountaineers and yak-chasers.

The butter tea is often mixed with tsampa, a roasted barley or wheat flour, to make a porridge. Alternatively, a spoonful of tsampa is mixed into the last drops of the tea so a little doughball treat can be scooped up and eaten. **GH**

Serves 4

Ingredients
4 teaspoons loose leaf breakfast
  tea (or 4 breakfast tea bags)
½ teaspoon sea salt
200ml (7fl oz) good quality
  whole milk
4 tablespoons Cultured Butter
  (page 140)

In a large pan over a medium-high heat, bring 750ml (25fl oz) water to the boil.

Add the tea and simmer for 2 minutes, then add the salt.

Remove from the heat and strain into a large bowl.

Return the liquid to the pan. Add the milk and butter to the tea and warm until steaming, but not boiling. Blitz with a stick blender until completely incorporated.

Serve immediately, with a hot buttered roll, fresh from the oven.

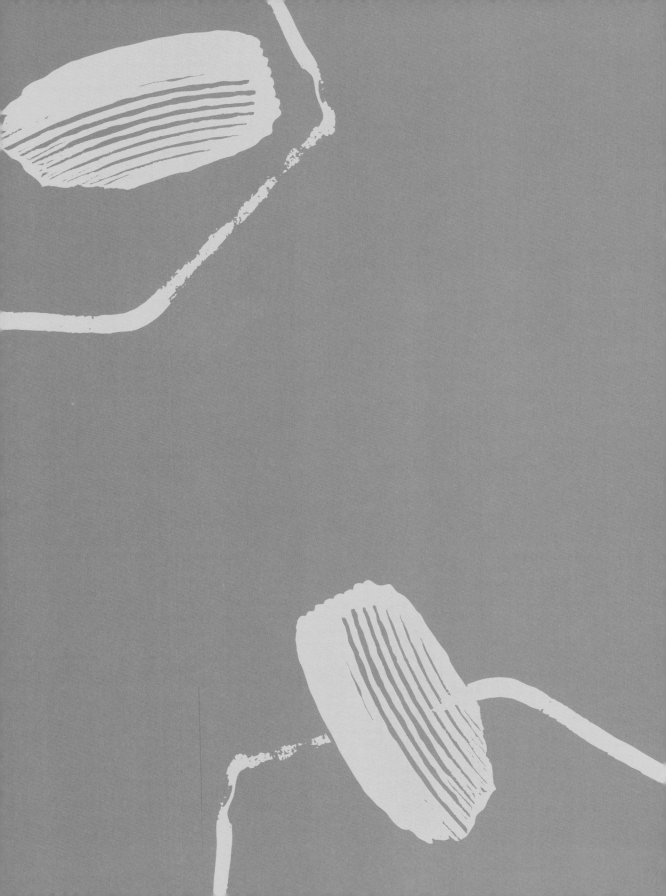

BREAD & BUTTER

Sandwiches

My first foray into the food world was as a 'sandwich artiste'. At the back of a pokey delicatessen in North Oxford, a small squad of us would stand armed with palette knives, ready to spread at the instruction of local office workers.

The counter in front of us was prepped with tubs of hummus, salami, semidried tomatoes, artichoke hearts, crispy salads and jar upon jar of obscure condiments. It was our responsibility to know the 'usuals' of the 'regulars', and heaven forbid if a certain local radio host was served his chicken mayo on a plain instead of seeded roll.

Sandwich artistry taught me many things: quick thinking, initiative and the popularity of pesto. But most importantly, it taught me the fail-safe rules for making a good sandwich: start with good bread, moisten with an appropriate spread, fill with something patty-esque, garnish with something crisp and season well, then serve immediately. Here are some of our timeless favourites, designed to please and comfort. **EH**

Grilled Cheese Sandwich

Yes, it is a lot of cheese. In the words of Mr Snapes himself, 'it has to be a lot, or there's no point'.

Makes 1

Ingredients
2 x 2cm (¾in) thick slices of
    sourdough bread
1–2 teaspoons Dijon mustard,
    to taste
150g (5oz) strong mature
    cheddar, such as Montgomery
    or Keen's, grated
Lashings of softened butter
pickles or hot sauce, to serve

Liberally spread one side of each slice of bread with the mustard.

Pile and squish all the cheese onto one slice of the mustard-spread bread and place the other slice on top, mustard-side down.

Slather the outside of the sandwich in butter.

Place a large non-stick frying pan over a medium-high heat. When the pan is good and hot, carefully place the sandwich in the pan. Apply pressure with a fish slice or spatula, so that the sandwich makes a 'tssssss' noise; if there's no noise, turn up the heat.

Cook until golden brown on the first side, approximately 2 minutes, then flip and apply pressure on the other side.

Keep flipping and applying pressure until it's ready. You'll know it's done when the whole sandwich is crispy and golden brown, and molten cheese is oozing through the holes in the bread.

Cut in half and serve with a tangy pickle or your choice of smoky hot sauce.

The Snapery Breakfast Sandwich

A regular occurrence at The Snapery Bakery, circa 9am, post-bake and mid-dough-shift, to give a burst of energy to a baker's day. Perfection when served with strong black coffee or freshly squeezed pink grapefruit juice.

Makes 1

Ingredients
splash of groundnut oil
2 slices of smoked streaky
  bacon
1 large egg
50g (1¾oz) mature cheddar
  cheese, sliced
1 brioche bun (page 122)
butter, to spread
2 splashes of hot sauce

Preheat the grill (broiler) to a high heat.

Drizzle the groundnut oil into a large frying pan and fry the bacon over a high heat until crispy. Add the egg to the pan and fry until it's crisp underneath but the yolk is still runny.

Place the cheese on top of the bacon in the pan so that it begins to melt.

Toast the brioche under the grill until just golden, keeping a close eye on it, as the sugar in the brioche means it can quickly burn. Butter the brioche thinly.

Place the cheesy bacon on the bottom of the brioche bun and top with the egg and a couple of generous splashes of hot sauce.

Close with the top of the brioche bun to complete this oozy, joyous mess of a sandwich.

Jambon Beurre Sandwich

A classic French baguette, so simple and satisfying. Found in most Parisian cafés and enjoyed by children and nostalgic adults alike.

Makes 1

Ingredients
hunk of baguette (page 97)
butter, to spread
salt flakes, to season
2 slices of thick-cut baked ham

Cut the baguette almost in half, so it's still joined on one side.

Liberally spread with butter and sprinkle salt flakes, to taste.

Fill with the ham and fold shut, then enjoy as part of a picnic or go solo for more authentic eating.

Steak Burger

Our version of an all-in burger. To turn into a butter burger, popular in Midwestern America, replace the cheese, bacon, lettuce and pickle with a 1cm (½in) slice of room temperature butter placed on the burger just before serving, letting the heat from the burger melt the butter before digging in.

Makes 1

Ingredients

125g (4½oz) rib-eye, chuck or any other fatty steak
splash of groundnut oil
2 rashers of smoked streaky bacon
1 brioche bun (page 122), buttered
1 tablespoon tomato ketchup
1–2 teaspoons American yellow mustard
1 iceberg lettuce leaf, shredded
1 large gherkin (dill pickle), sliced
1 slice of Emmental cheese
sea salt flakes and cracked black pepper

For the chipotle mayo
1 dried chipotle chilli
1½ tablespoons mayonnaise

Start by making the chipotle mayo. Soak the chilli in hot water for 5 minutes, then remove and chop finely. Stir about half of it into the mayonnaise, then add more to taste – the flavour will develop over time, so don't go overboard initially.

Next, make the burger. Cut the steak into tiny chunks as if you were making a mirepoix (there's no need to be overly precise). If you're lucky enough to own a mincer, mince away on a coarse setting. Shape the steak into a burger roughly 1cm (½in) thick and 7½cm (3in) wide.

Heat the groundnut oil in a large frying pan over a high heat. At the same time, preheat the grill (broiler) to a high heat. When you sense good sizzle action, fry the bacon until the fat is foaming on each rasher, then take out of the pan and drain on kitchen paper to crisp further. Leave the bacon fat in the pan to fry the burger.

Season the outside of your burger with plenty of salt and pepper, then place in the pan and cook over a medium-high for 1½ minutes on each side. You'll need to assemble your other sandwich elements as soon as you've flipped, so these next steps will go quite quickly...

Slice the bun in half and toast under the grill: keep an eye on it, as brioche toasts in moments and you want it toasted, not torched. Butter the bun.

Sauce dispersion will always be a contentious issue (between us, we couldn't even agree on one method for this book!). My preferred combination is to spread the chipotle mayo on both sides of the bun and then dollop ketchup on one side and mustard on the other, but feel free to go your own way. Place the lettuce and gherkin on the bottom half of the bun. Once the burger has been flipped, place the bacon on top of it, followed by the cheese, and cook for another minute.

Now place a heatproof bowl over the burger pile while it's still in the pan, to trap steam for a moist burger and cheesy, melty goodness – if it seems too dry, splash a little water under the bowl. Cook for another 30 seconds. Carefully transfer the burger pile to the bottom half of the bun, place the other half on top and eat with both hands.

Charred Broccoli & Stracciatella di Bufala

Confusingly, stracciatella can be three foods in Italy: a cheese, an ice cream or an egg drop soup. This sandwich uses the cheese (trust me, it really wouldn't be nice with either of the other two), and it goes perfectly with a handful of garlic-marinated olives or a pungent salami beer stick. You could also use burrata or mozzarella if stracciatella is not available.

Makes 1

Ingredients
5 stems of Tenderstem broccoli
1 tablespoon extra virgin olive oil
2 x 2cm (¾in) thick slices of
    sourdough bread
lashings of softened butter
50g (1¾oz) stracciatella di bufala
    cheese (alternatively use
    burrata or mozzarella)
sea salt and freshly ground
    black pepper
squeeze of lemon juice

Put a large griddle pan over a high heat.

Toss the broccoli in the olive oil and season with salt and pepper.

When the griddle pan is hot and you're confident you'll get a good sizzle, lay the bread slices and broccoli in the pan.

When the bread has nice char lines across it on one side, take it out of the pan, then flip the broccoli so it chars on both sides.

Butter the non-charred side of each slice of bread. Spoon the stracciatella cheese on to one slice, then place the charred broccoli on top. Season with pepper and lemon juice.

Place the other slice of bread on top, butter-side down, cut in half and serve.

Sourdough Treacle Tart

I first tried sourdough treacle tart at Silo in Brighton, I don't know why I hadn't thought of it before – a classic recipe, staying true to the age-old ethic of using up old bread, but doing it in a more delicious way. It goes without saying that this is a very sweet dessert. I've offset it here with a lot of lemon, and the tang of the sourdough also goes some way to balancing it, but ultimately this is for those with a really sweet tooth. **RS**

Serves 8–10

Ingredients
300g (10½oz) golden syrup
100g (3½oz) maple syrup
125g (4½oz) breadcrumbs,
    made from day-old sourdough
    bread (without crusts)
finely grated zest and juice of
    1 large lemon
large knob of butter
cultured or clotted cream, to
    serve (optional)

*For the pastry (this makes twice
    as much as you need)*
100g (3½oz) cold butter, diced
230g (8oz) plain (all-purpose)
    flour, extra for dusting
120g (4oz) caster (superfine)
    sugar
1 large egg, lightly beaten

First make the pastry. Rub the butter into the flour and sugar with your fingertips, then gradually add the egg until just coming together (be careful not to overwork the pastry or it will become tough). Form your dough into a rough ball and cut in half. Cover both halves with plastic wrap/clingfilm and pop one in the freezer, for use at a later date, and chill one in the fridge for 30 minutes.

Preheat the oven to 190°C (375°F). Take your pastry out of the fridge and roll out on a lightly floured surface so that it it's big enough to fit a 18–20cm (7–8in) tart tin with some overhang. Transfer the pastry to your butter-greased tart tin and use your fingers to carefully push the pastry into the sides – don't worry about any pastry overhang as we'll trim that later to make it look nice.

Line the tart case with baking paper and fill with baking beans or uncooked rice, then blind-bake for 15 minutes. While the pastry is baking, make the filling.

In a large saucepan over a low heat, gently warm the golden syrup and maple syrup until loose and runny – take care not to let it boil or the sugars will burn. Take off the heat and add the breadcrumbs, lemon zest and juice and the butter. Stir until the breadcrumbs have absorbed the syrup.

Remove the paper and beans from the tart case and bake for a further 5 minutes to dry out the base of the tart case. Take the tart case out of the oven, then turn the temperature down to 160°C (320°F).

With a sharp knife, carefully trim the overhanging edges of the tart case. Pour the filling into the tart case and bake for 25–30 minutes, until a deep, golden colour. Serve with cultured or clotted cream to give your arteries an extra challenge.

Brioche & Brown Butter Ice Cream

Given the amount of butter in this book, it's tough to say which recipe is the most decadent. For sure, Buttermilk Fried Quails (page 228) is a strong contender, but ultimately it has to be this ice cream. I'm not sure how it could be any butterier. Firstly, there's butter in the brioche crumbs; then there's the burnt butter that gets whizzed into the custard; and lastly, we gently fry brioche in butter to add some chewy chunks to the ice cream. If Mr Creosote were to eat ice cream, this would be his first choice.

The recipe makes two tubs: one for digging into as soon as it's frozen and one for forgetting about, so that when you're craving something sweet and remember you have this in the freezer, you can feel very pleased with yourself. This was one of the first recipes we invented when we decided on a book about bread and butter, I suppose it's our attempt at giving brown-bread ice cream, a popular dinner party dessert in the 1970s, a little facelift – and I have a very soft spot for it... right around my abdomen. **EH**

Make sure to blend the brown butter in at top speed to prevent the texture of the ice cream becoming grainy.

Makes 2 x 350ml (12⅓fl oz) tubs

Equipment
food processor
ice-cream maker

Ingredients
300ml (10½fl oz) whole
    unhomogenised milk
145g (5oz) Brioche (page 122)
4 egg yolks
80g (3oz) golden caster
    (superfine) sugar
150ml (5fl oz) double (thick)
    cream
1 teaspoon vanilla extract
pinch of salt
75g (2½oz) Cultured Butter
    (page 140)

Gently heat the milk in a pan on a low heat until steaming hot. Do not let it get hotter than this – if it looks like it's coming to the boil, take it off the heat and leave to cool for a minute or two.

Weigh out 90g (3¼) of the brioche and remove the crusts so you're left with 50g (1¾oz) crustless brioche. Blitz to fine breadcrumbs in a food processor and put to one side.

In a large bowl, whisk the egg yolks and sugar for a couple of minutes until well combined – the sugar will begin to dissolve but the mixture will still be a little grainy. Keep whisking as you add the warm milk: you want to do this really slowly to stop the hot milk from cooking the eggs. You really don't want to end up with watery scrambled eggs.

When all the milk is incorporated, pour the custard back into the milk pan. Return to a medium-low heat and cook, stirring, for 8–10 minutes, by which time the custard should have thickened slightly.

Now transfer the custard to the food processor, along with the breadcrumbs, cream, vanilla extract and salt, and blitz briefly – the cool cream and air will prevent the custard from cooking any further.

Put 50g (1¾oz) of the butter in a small frying pan and melt over a medium-high heat until the white milk solids turn a chocolate Labrador shade of brown, smell sweet and sink to the bottom of the pan. I like to add these caramelised milk solids to the ice cream – they give a lovely colour, and the slightly burnt

bitterness offsets some of the richness. This is personal preference though, so do feel free to sieve the milk solids out of your brown butter before adding it to the custard, if you'd prefer.

With your food processor whizzing on full blast, slowly add the brown butter to the custard. It's very important to keep the custard moving when you add the butter, or the ice cream will go grainy when frozen.

When all the brown butter is added, chill the custard overnight in the fridge.

The next day, slice the rest of your brioche into 1cm (½in) slices and butter on both sides with the remaining butter.

Place the buttered slices of brioche into a hot, medium frying pan and fry over a medium heat until they are golden brown – they will burn quickly, so be sure to keep a good eye on them. Chop the fried brioche into rough chunks – and nibble a few for 'cook's treats'…

You're now ready to churn the ice cream. Churn as per your ice-cream maker's instructions, adding chunks of fried brioche as you go.

Transfer the ice cream to two pre-chilled tubs labelled 'now' and 'later' and enjoy at the appropriate time.

Bread & Butter Pickles

This is the only recipe in the book that contains neither bread nor butter. In that sense, it is a fraud of a recipe, but the pickles are so delicious I think we will have to let it slide. There are several schools of thought surrounding the name. Some say that an American couple survived the Depression by making these pickles and bartering with them for staples such as bread and butter. Others say that people used to eat these pickles between bread and butter as a sandwich as they were too poor for something more substantial. Either way, I'm glad they were invented. It can be very difficult to find cornichons to pickle, you can grow them yourself but this really is a lot to ask. It's easier to buy Lebanese ones, which are shorter and thinner versions of regular cucumbers and work very well for pickling. This recipe intentionally makes a little too much pickling liquor so that you can quick pickle something on the side to have as a snack. Apples and pears work particularly well but you could also try daikon, radishes or kohlrabi. **EH**

Fills a 500ml (17fl oz) jar

Ingredients
3–4 small cucumbers or
    fresh cornichons (approx.
    400g/14oz)
2–3 shallots (approx.
    100g/3½oz)
2 tablespoons rock salt
1 large garlic clove
1 teaspoon white mustard seeds
½ teaspoon fennel seed
½ teaspoon ground turmeric
100g (3½oz) white caster
    (superfine) sugar
300ml (10½fl oz) unpasteurised,
    unfiltered apple cider vinegar

You can either cut the cucumbers into slices and put them in a flat-bottomed dish, or if you're using cornichons, then place them whole in a flat-bottomed dish.

Peel and finely slice the shallots and add them to the cucumbers. Sprinkle the salt over the cucumbers and shallots. Then cover with plastic wrap/clingfilm and place a weight, I usually use a few heavy dishes, on top of the cucumbers. We're trying to draw out some of the moisture here, and the weight will help to do that. Leave the cucumbers overnight in the refrigerator.

The next day, peel and finely slice the garlic. Add it to a small saucepan with the mustard seeds, fennel, turmeric and sugar. Pour in the vinegar and gently heat until simmering. Simmer for 5 minutes and then take the cucumbers from the fridge and pour all the liquid over the cucumbers. Stir gently and then pack the cucumbers into an appropriate-sized jar. The jar should be clean but you do not need to sterilise it as the pickling liquor is sufficiently acidic to make it safe for storing food.

You should have just under half the pickling liquor remaining. Chop your favourite crunchy fruit or veg, toss in a little salt and coat in the leftover liquor. The bread and butter pickles can also be eaten straight away, but they are much better left for a week. They will keep for around 3 weeks.

Bread Sauce

I remember bread sauce being served with a Sunday roast at my friend Ellie's house when we were children. It was very exciting to have two sauces to go with my chicken. Liquid bread just seemed to me a perfect excuse to eat more bread. Here is my grown-up version of a childishly comforting dish. **EH**

Makes 600ml (21fl oz), serves 4

Ingredients
1 medium onion
4 whole cloves
1 large bay leaf
5 black peppercorns
500ml (17fl oz) organic
    whole milk
100g (3½oz) stale sourdough
    bread
2 tablespoons double
    (thick)cream
15g (½oz) butter
a grating of nutmeg

Peel and quarter the onion and stud each quarter with a clove.

Place the onion quarters, bay leaf and peppercorns in a medium saucepan. Add the milk and warm over a medium heat for 25 minutes. Don't let the milk catch or boil, just keep it warm enough to release a little steam, which is hot enough to allow the milk to infuse with the aromatics.

In the meantime, chop the bread into very small pieces. I tend to keep the crusts, but feel free to remove if you're afraid your hair will curl, just make sure to keep the 100g (3½oz) weight as outlined in the ingredient list.

When the milk is steeped, remove the onion and peppercorns by straining the milk through a sieve. Reserve the milk and the bay leaf.

Return the milk and bay leaf to the pan and add the bread. Cook the sauce until the bread has disintegrated and the texture is similar to porridge.

Then add the cream, butter and nutmeg and stir. The cream and butter will loosen the mixture slightly making it ready to pour over your roast chicken, potatoes or Yorkshire pudding.

Bagna Cauda

I don't own a fondue set, mainly to prevent myself from eating ludicrous quantities of liquid cheese, but if I did, I would make bagna cauda even more than I do already. Bagna cauda, from the Italian, *bagno caldo* meaning 'hot bath', is best served with fresh, crunchy bitter vegetables that can compete with the pungent garlic and anchovy-laden sauce. This maybe isn't one for a first date, or maybe it is! I wouldn't want to date anyone who would balk at a fishy bread dip.

I understand it's common to serve bagna cauda as you would a fondue, so this recipe is an excuse the get your fondue set out and enjoy a dip of something a little less cheesey and a bit more Piedmontese-y. **EH**

Serves 6 as a starter

Ingredients
1 bulb garlic
350ml (12¹/₃fl oz) organic
 whole milk
70g (2½oz) stale sourdough
 bread
100g (3½oz) jar good-quality
 anchovies in oil
2 teaspoons white wine vinegar
100g (3½oz) butter
pinch white ground pepper
raw, crisp and cold chicories,
 fennel, radishes and celery
 (or more bread if you desire),
 to serve

Peel the garlic and place in a medium saucepan along with the milk. Heat gently on a low heat for 30 minutes. Be careful not to let it boil, as it may curdle, which wouldn't be the end of the world, but doesn't look particularly appetising.

Meanwhile, finely chop the bread. Drain the anchovies, reserving the oil from the jar, and finely chop. The more finely you chop, the quicker your bagna cauda will cook. If you're very impatient, you can take the crusts off your bread as they take the longest to cook down, but I'd recommend leaving them on as they give a lovely depth of flavour.

When the garlic milk mixture is ready, use a potato masher to squash the cloves into the milk. Then add the bread and anchovies, as well as the oil from the anchovy jar. Cook for a further 15 minutes, or until the bread has absorbed all of the milk and oil. You should be left with a very thick mixture.

Add the vinegar, butter and white pepper to the mixture and stir well. At this point, the dip should turn glossy.

Prepare the vegetables ready for the hot dip. Serve the dip with the veg, making sure it's within arm's reach of everyone involved.

Brioche & Butter Pudding

I'm always amazed to find so many people still repulsed by childhood memories of bread and butter pudding as a sloppy, bland mess made with the cheapest sliced white. Let's be clear, the only place for sliced white is a bacon sarnie with brown sauce. When it comes to bread and butter pudding – or in this case, brioche and butter pudding – the bread needs to have substance. With a little care, some leftover *real* bread and some chocolatey gems, this will stand up well against any pudding. You're aiming for golden crispiness on the edges with spiced, custardy goodness inside. **RS**

Serves 4–6

Ingredients
1 Earl Grey tea bag
125g (4½oz) sultanas (golden raisins)
50g (1¾oz) 100% cocoa chocolate (or as dark as you can find)
3 large eggs
60g (2oz) caster (superfine) sugar
1 teaspoon vanilla extract
225ml (8fl oz) whole milk
100ml (3½fl oz) double (thick) cream
400g (14oz) stale brioche
60g (2oz) salted butter, extra for greasing
whole nutmeg, for grating
1 tablespoon demerara sugar
cream or ice cream, to serve

Brew the tea bag in 500ml (17fl oz) boiling water, then cool for 10 minutes. Add the sultanas and leave to soak for a minimum of 2 hours, or preferably overnight in the fridge.

Roughly chop the chocolate into drawing-pin-sized chunks.

Whisk together the eggs, caster sugar and vanilla extract, then pour in the milk and cream and whisk until you have a smooth custard mixture.

Slice the brioche into 1cm (½in) slices and spread with the butter.

And now for the fun part. Somehow, anything in layers tastes better – lasagne, tiramisu, parmigiana – and this pudding is no exception. Generously butter a rectangular, ovenproof dish, about 40cm x 25cm (16in x 10in), and line with slices of buttered brioche. Dot with the soaked sultanas and the chocolate, then saturate with the custard mixture. Repeat these layers until everything is used up – you should have 3 or 4 layers.

Using your hands, gently squish the pudding to help the brioche absorb all of the delicious liquid. Grate nutmeg liberally over the top and scatter with the demerara sugar, then set aside for 30 minutes to allow the brioche to absorb the custard.

Preheat the oven to 180°C (350°F) and bake the pudding for 35–40 minutes until dark golden brown. Serve warm with cream or ice cream.

LEFTOVERS

Panzanella

This is by no means an authentic version of a classic Tuscan bread salad, but a book about bread just wouldn't be complete without some kind of salute to the rustic ripped-bread tradition. Of course, there is no right or wrong way to make panzanella. In Italian cookbooks, recipes will often simply say 'quanto basta' – 'as much as is enough' – which is simultaneously frustrating and liberating. For us, panzanella can be a dish for when there is little in the cupboards but old bread, some squishy tomatoes and a can of anchovies. But the spicier version below is a sure-fire way to transport you to sunnier climes. **EH**

Serves 3

Ingredients
1 red (bell) pepper
5 tablespoons extra virgin
    olive oil
½ teaspoon cumin seeds
150g (5oz) stale bread (ciabatta
    or baguette work well, but
    sourdough is also fine)
3 garlic cloves, 2 bruised,
    1 finely chopped
400g (14oz) ripe tomatoes
    (mixed colours), roughly
    chopped
½ teaspoon smoked paprika
    (or rehydrated and finely
    chopped dried chipotle chilli)
2 teaspoons red wine vinegar
2 teaspoons capers
large bunch of basil, leaves
    picked
large bunch of flat-leaf parsley,
    leaves picked and roughly
    chopped
sea salt and freshly ground
    black pepper

Preheat the oven to 180°C (350°F).

Put the whole red pepper into a roasting tin with 1 tablespoon olive oil and the cumin seeds. Season with salt and pepper, then roast in the oven for 20–30 minutes until juicy and blackened.

Meanwhile, cut the bread into 1cm (½in) cubes and throw onto a baking tray along with the bruised garlic cloves. If your bread is more than a day old and is quite stale and dry, sprinkle over a little water. Drizzle the bread with 2 tablespoons olive oil and toast in the oven for 10–12 minutes until golden brown and crispy.

Put your tomatoes into a large bowl. Mix in a good pinch of salt, the finely chopped garlic clove and the smoked paprika, then leave for 10–15 minutes. The salt will draw out some of the moisture from the tomatoes – drain this liquid off, reserving it to make the dressing.

In a small bowl, whisk together the remaining 2 tablespoons olive oil, the red wine vinegar and 2 tablespoons of the tomato liquid. Taste and adjust the seasoning with salt, pepper and tomato liquid until you have a satisfyingly salty, tangy and smoky dressing.

Now it's time to assemble the salad. Crumble a few of the croutons and mix them in with the tomatoes to soak up any more liquid that has seeped out from them. Tear the roast pepper into strips and add to the bowl, along with the capers, basil leaves, parsley and the remaining croutons. Finallly, drizzle with your dressing and serve immediately, while the croutons are still crunchy.

Pappa al Pomodoro

I wholeheartedly agree with David Rosengarten when he amusingly wrote that, to Tuscans, 'the pappa is little more than an excuse for eating olive oil'. Best served at room temperature as an appetiser with good glugs of your best olive oil, it happily sits alongside most Mediterranean-style meals.

Although the dish only takes about 20 minutes to make, please, please allow a good few hours (or preferably a whole day) before you intend to serve it. As with most allium-heavy dishes, the flavours mellow over time, and your patience will be rewarded with a much deeper and more satisfying flavour. This recipe could also be easily adapted into a summer soup by increasing the number of tomatoes or adding some good-quality vegetable stock. **EH**

Serves 2

Ingredients
40g (1½oz) stale bread, thickly sliced
2 very ripe tomatoes, diced
3 tablespoons good-quality extra virgin olive oil, plus extra to serve
2 large garlic cloves, finely chopped or crushed
½ red chilli, finely chopped
2 tablespoons tomato purée
about 10 basil leaves
sea salt and freshly ground black pepper

Toast the bread and tear into marshmallow-sized chunks.

Put the tomatoes in a bowl, along with any juices from the chopping board.

Heat the olive oil in a frying pan over a medium-low heat and add the garlic and chilli. After 2–3 minutes, when the garlic is aromatic (but not browned), add the tomatoes and the tomato purée. Stir well.

When the tomatoes have begun to break down, add the chunks of bread and basil leaves and keep stirring. The consistency will depend on how juicy your tomatoes are and how absorbent your bread is. Sourdough tends to be very absorbent, so you might need to add a little water at this point to keep it saucy.

Cook for another 5 minutes, then take off the heat and leave in the pan until you are ready to serve. This should be no less than an hour away, but ideally the next day. By then, the garlic and chilli will have mellowed and the whole dish should hum beautifully.

Serve in small bowls, drizzled with a little more olive oil.

Bread Pudding

Mrs Beeton's Book of Household Management has no less than four recipes for bread pudding. Ranging from a 'very plain bread pudding' (how appetising, Mrs Beeton!) to a 'brown bread pudding' that one must 'boil for nearly four hours'. Finding it a little tricky to get enthused about these austere recipes, I decided to make a version packed with fruit that's perfect for when you fancy baking something, but have run out of flour and can't be bothered to go to the shops.

For the bread component, I used spelt sourdough; wholemeal breads give a deeper flavour, but white would also be fine if that's what you have. I like to keep the crusts on for added texture, but if you prefer a smoother pudding, feel free to remove them. I also stuck with tradition and left the suet in there, but this could easily be replaced with the same amount of melted butter to make a veggie-friendly pudding. **EH**

Serves 6

75g (2½oz) dried figs, roughly chopped
50g (1¾oz) sultanas (golden raisins)
50g (1¾oz) candied mixed peel
25g (1oz) dates, roughly chopped
25g (1oz) dried cranberries
2 English Breakfast tea bags
200g (7oz) slightly stale sourdough bread
300ml (10½fl oz) whole milk
finely grated zest of 1 orange
30g (1oz) suet
1 large egg, lightly beaten
50g (1¾oz) caster (superfine) sugar
1½ teaspoons mixed spice
½ teaspoon ground cinnamon
whole nutmeg, for grating
2 tablespoons demerara sugar
cream or custard, to serve

Start by soaking the fruit. Put all the dried fruit into a heatproof bowl. Brew 250ml (8¾fl oz) strong black tea with the 2 tea bags, then pour over the fruit and leave to steep for about an hour, but preferably overnight.

Chop or tear the bread into small bite-sized pieces. Place the bread in a wide, flat-bottomed dish, pour over the milk and leave to soak for an hour.

Preheat the oven to 180°C (350°F) and lightly butter a baking dish about 30cm x 20cm (12in x 8in).

The bread should have soaked up most, if not all, of the milk. Drain off any excess, then take a fork and mash the soggy bread into a rough pulp. Drain (and reserve) any tea that hasn't been absorbed by the dried fruit, then mix the orange zest, suet, egg, caster sugar, mixed spice and cinnamon with the fruit.

Add the fruit mixture to the bread mixture, and mix thoroughly. The texture should be like a very thick batter – not quite pourable but easily spoonable. If it seems a little too solid, add some of the reserved tea to loosen it up.

Transfer to the baking dish and level the pudding with the back of a spoon. Grate some nutmeg over the top and bake for 1 hour 10 minutes, checking it after an hour. When it's done, it should be a dark chocolatey colour on top and just set (but still soft) in the middle. Sprinkle with the demerara sugar while it's still warm.

Ribollita Fritters

Ribollita is most commonly described as a Tuscan bean and vegetable soup. Soup, as I'm sure you're aware, normally comes in bowls, is liquid and eaten with spoons. During our research for this book, all the pictures of ribollita we came across in cookbooks complied with the viscous nature of the dish. And yet, when I ordered it for the first time in a Tuscan restaurant, I was presented with a large dinner plate. In the middle was a brownish-grey mound that closely resembled one of my expertly crafted mud pies from 1994. Somewhat apprehensively, I clutched my fork and scooped up some sludge, much as if it were a miniature trowel making a dent in newly turned dirt. But when I placed the ribollita in my mouth I was amazed to discover that such a rustic dish could be so packed full of flavour. It was delicate, aromatic and comforting.

Of course, I gobbled the whole lot and then demanded to talk to the chef so I could learn his secret. The chef came over to the table, shaking his head: this was not possible, he could not tell us, and we would have to leave with only our appetites satisfied, not our curiosity… unless, he added, we could come back the next morning, so he could show us in person.

Needless to say, we returned. There was a table laid out for us and we were promptly presented with an onion lasagne (made from layers of onion and bread) – but this was not the ribollita I was so desperate to uncover the secrets of. We duly praised the lasagne and made all the right noises so we could get into the kitchen. This recipe is based on what was told to us that day.

The key thing here is to plan ahead: the vegetable base must be cooked for a minimum of three hours, and then the ribollita mixture needs to sit overnight. Deep flavours need time to develop, and you cannot rush them. You can afford to be flexible when it comes to the ingredients, since this dish is often comprised of whatever vegetables are to hand, but the long, slow cooking is non-negotiable. The traditional Tuscan bread used to make ribollita is dry and unseasoned, but I enjoy the spongy texture given by sourdough – use whichever is to your personal taste. **EH**

>>

**Serves 4 as a main,
or 6 as a starter**

Ingredients
125g (4½oz) dried or
   1 x 400g/14oz can cannellini
   or flageolet beans
1 white onion
2 carrots
1 large celery stick
125g (4½oz) cavolo nero
2 potatoes
400g (14oz) ripe tomatoes
3 large garlic cloves
bunch of flat-leaf parsley
8 tablespoons extra virgin
   olive oil
1 heaped tablespoon
   tomato purée
1 large bay leaf
bunch of thyme, leaves picked
100g (3½oz) stale bread, sliced
sea salt and freshly ground
   black pepper
frisée salad, to serve

Prepare your beans. If cooking from dried, soak the beans overnight, then bring a medium pan of fresh unsalted water to a simmer and cook the beans for 30–40 minutes until soft. If using canned, simmer the contents of the tin for 5 minutes, adding a little extra water if needed to make sure the beans are well covered.

Using a slotted spoon, take half of the beans out of the cooking water and set aside. Keep enough of the bean-cooking water in the saucepan with the remaining beans to just cover them, then blitz with a stick blender or food processor until you have a thin liquid. Put this to one side as well.

Next, prepare your vegetables. Cut the onion, carrots, celery, cavolo nero, potatoes and tomatoes into humbug-sized chunks, keeping them all separate. Finely slice the garlic and parsley, including the stems.

Heat half of the olive oil in a large saucepan over a medium heat and, when it's hot but not smoking, add the onion and cook for 15 minutes. It should be translucent and starting to caramelise, but don't let it go too brown and sticky.

Add the carrots, celery, half of the cavolo nero, potatoes, garlic, half of the parsley, tomato paste, bay leaf and thyme leaves and continue to cook for 10 minutes, making sure everything is glistening in olive oil – you may need to add another drizzle.

Add the tomatoes and the blitzed beans and bring to a simmer. Turn the heat down as low as it will go, then cover and cook for a minimum of 3 hours, but preferably 4–5, stirring occasionally. If it starts to stick or gets too dry, add a little water to keep it bubbling nicely. At 20 minutes before the end of cooking, add the remaining beans, cavolo nero and parsley. Season and stir well.

When the vegetables are done, take a large lidded dish and alternately layer the vegetable mix with the bread, finishing with a layer of the vegetable mix. Cover the ribollita and leave at room temperature overnight: the vegetable mix will soak into the bread to form a relatively solid mass.

The next day, when you're ready for lunch or dinner (or breakfast – there's no judgement here), heat the remaining olive oil in a frying pan over a medium heat. When it's hot, carve out a large, serving-spoon-sized spoonful of the ribollita and place in the pan, gently flattening it into a more fritter-like shape with the back of the spoon.

Add another 3 spoonfuls to the pan and cook the fritters for 5 minutes on each side, turning with a fish slice, until they're super-crispy all over.

Serve immediately. Although the fritters may look small, they're substantial, and you'll need little more than a crisp frisée salad to accompany them. Any remaining ribollita mixture will keep for a few days in the fridge and will improve over that time.

Açorda de Gambas

We tried this dish in a wonderful restaurant in Lisbon. It's a kind of bread soup, aromatic with coriander, rich with egg and oil, and thick and comforting. We spoke to the chef afterwards, who advised us the secret is really a lot of olive oil (from the little pools on top, not such a secret), and the recipe we have replicated below is based on his advice. There are different variations, but topping with prawns is common – or try flash-frying a scallop per person and placing on top. **EH**

Makes 2–3 servings

Ingredients
125g (4½oz) stale sourdough bread
1 bulb garlic
5 tablespoons extra virgin olive oil
25g (1oz) coriander
1 tablespoon white wine vinegar
125g (4½oz) uncooked king prawn (shrimp), or 1 scallop, per person
2 egg yolks
1 teaspoon chilli flakes (optional)
Sea salt and ground white pepper

Cut the bread into 1cm (½in) cubes. You can leave the crusts on or off. I prefer to leave mine on, the soup takes a little longer to cook but it means no unnecessary waste. If the bread is fresh then place the cubes under the grill (broiler) for a few moments to dehydrate the bread, but don't toast it. If it is stale, use as is.

Preheat the oven to 180°C (350°F). Cut the top off the garlic bulb so you can see cross-sections of each clove if you look down on it from above. Put the bulb in a small roasting tray and pour 1 tablespoon olive oil into the bulb slowly so the oil trickles between the cloves. Roast the bulb for 20 minutes.

In the meantime, take the leaves off the coriander and finely chop the stalks. When the garlic is ready, hook each clove out of the bulb with a fork.

In a medium saucepan, warm 2 tablespoons olive oil over a medium heat. Gently fry the roasted garlic, half the coriander leaves and the coriander stalks for 2 minutes before adding the bread. Stir, then add a little salt and pepper. Next, add 500ml (17fl oz) water and the vinegar, and bring to a simmer. Cook for 15 minutes until porridge-like, you may need to add a little more water to keep it liquid, but it should be very thick.

While the soup is cooking, prepare the prawns. Lightly coat in 1 tablespoon olive oil and season. Get a frying pan nice and hot before popping the seafood in, cook for a minute on each side. Decant to a plate.

Before serving, stir the remaining coriander leaves and egg yolks into the soup. Check the seasoning. Then divide the soup into bowls and top with the prawns and chilli flakes, for an extra kick. Wash down with a little white port.

Buttermilk Fried Quails

Quail is a perfect bird to deep-fry whole. Their size means that, with care, they cook through evenly and provide plenty of little crispy edges. Quails are normally available in any good butchers, but the time of the year they are most flavoursome will vary, depending on where you are in the world: in the UK, they're at their best in early autumn, whereas in North America, you'll want to wait until the end of the year. And if you can't find quail, or you're after a vegetarian version, this recipe also works perfectly with cauliflower quarters.

When deep-frying, you'll need to make sure your pan is large enough for all the birds to be submerged in the oil; if not, cook them one at a time. **GH**

Serves 4

Equipment
digital thermometer

Ingredients
4 quails
4 teaspoons sea salt
500ml (17fl oz) buttermilk
3 litres (3 quarts) groundnut
  or sunflower oil
150g (5oz) plain (all-purpose)
  flour
2 teaspoons brown sugar
1 teaspoon dried oregano
1 teaspoon dried sage
1 teaspoon dried basil
1 teaspoon dried marjoram
1 teaspoon gound white pepper
1 teaspoon ground black pepper
1 teaspoon chilli powder
1 teaspoon paprika
1 teaspoon onion powder
coleslaw and Bread and Butter
  Pickles (page 204),
  to serve

First, marinate the quails. Place the birds in a dish large enough to hold them all. Whisk 2 teaspoons of the salt into the buttermilk and pour over the quails, then cover and leave to marinate for at least 2 hours, but ideally overnight, in the fridge.

In a large heavy-based pan or deep-fryer, heat the oil to 180ºC (350ºF). If you don't have a digital thermometer, drop a small piece of bread into the hot oil – if it sizzles, the oil is ready, if it doesn't, wait a bit longer and test again.

Put the flour, spices, herbs, sugar and the remaining salt into a wide, shallow dish and mix well.

Drain the excess buttermilk from the quails. Taking one at a time, thoroughly coat in the flour mix before carefully lowering into the hot oil. When all the quails are in the oil, deep-fry for 9 minutes, or until golden and crispy.

Lift the quails out of the oil and drain on kitchen paper.

Serve immediately, ideally with slaw and Bread and Butter Pickles – and plenty of napkins.

Pecorino & Chilli Stuffing

A good while ago, when Rich and I first started dating, I did something pretty creepy. Every time we went on a date, or cooked a meal for each other, I wrote down what we'd eaten. Most of our interactions involved some kind of delicious meal, and I didn't want to forget them! I already knew we had a connection and, more pressingly, that there was a lot I could learn about food from this man. And so my inner nerd took over, giving in to my note-taking urges and methodically recording all our shared meals from those early days of our relationship.

Sobrasada baked in honey was the first entry in my notebook, then petits pois à la Française kept us ticking along nicely, but it was this home-made pecorino and chilli stuffing, served with roast chicken and greens, that sealed the deal. **EH**

Serves 6 as a side dish, or 4 as a starter

Ingredients
olive oil, for frying
large knob of butter
1 large onion, diced
4 garlic cloves, thinly sliced
1 red chilli, thinly sliced
4 sprigs thyme, leaves picked
200g (7oz) stale bread, crusts removed
300g (10½oz) good-quality sausage meat or de-skinned sausages
75g (2½oz) pecorino, grated
finely grated zest of 1 lemon
handful of flat-leaf parsley, chopped
200ml (7fl oz) chicken stock
sea salt and freshly ground black pepper

Preheat the oven to 200°C (400°F).

Put a large frying pan over a medium heat. Add a splash of olive oil and the butter, then fry the onion, garlic and chilli until soft and golden. Add the thyme leaves to the pan, then take off the heat. Transfer to a large bowl and leave to cool for a few minutes.

Cut the bread into 2cm (¾in) cubes, then blitz to coarse breadcrumbs in a food processor.

Tip the breadcrumbs into the bowl containing the onion, along with the sausage meat, pecorino, lemon zest and parsley and season. Slowly add the chicken stock: depending on the kind of bread you're using and how stale it is, you might not need it all, so start with 200ml (7fl oz) and add more if you think it needs it. The consistency should be just stiff enough to roll into balls.

Butter a 30cm x 20cm (12in x 8in) baking tray and fill with the stuffing. Dimple with a spoon so the surface resembles a ploughed field, then bake for 25–30 minutes until crispy and golden.

Best Buttermilk Dressing

This dressing has a real punch to it, from both the garlic and the acidity of the buttermilk. It's particularly good drizzled over crunchy iceberg lettuce scattered with some blue cheese and candied walnuts. **GH**

Makes 330ml (12fl oz) enough to dress a salad for 6

Ingredients
1 teaspoon paprika
1 teaspoon onion powder
1 garlic clove, finely chopped
juice and grated zest of ½ lemon
100ml (3½fl oz) mayonnaise
225ml (8fl oz) buttermilk
1 tablespoon chopped flat-leaf
   parsley
1 teaspoon chopped chives
sea salt and freshly ground
   black pepper

Mix the paprika, onion powder, garlic and a pinch of the lemon zest in a bowl.

Stir in 1 teaspoon of the lemon juice, together with the mayonnaise and buttermilk, then season with salt and pepper to taste. Adjust the acidity with more lemon if required.

Fold in the herbs just before serving.

Home Brewed Bread Beer

I invite you to think about sandwiches for a moment: all those sandwiches you see lined up on the refrigerated shelves of supermarkets, cafés and delis, satisfyingly symmetrical, with their enticing fillings peeking out. But have you ever thought about the bread used to make those sandwiches? How they're always constructed using 'normal' slices of bread, never the slice from the end of the loaf? So then, what happens to the thousands upon thousands of stubby end slices? In the majority of cases, the answer is nothing. And often both the end (heel) slice and the first slice are thrown away, which means that close to 17% of each loaf is wasted.

Because bread is typically cheap and relatively easy to mass-produce, it is one of the biggest sources of food waste worldwide. The latest estimates suggest that 44% of bread in the UK is wasted, with bread coming in as the second-most-wasted food in Europe (potatoes occupy the number one spot). As we're aiming to celebrate bread and butter in this book, I don't want to delve too deeply here, but it feels important to look at the bigger picture and talk about waste – which brings us neatly to the team at Toast, who make their beer using leftover bread.

I was first introduced to Rob, Louisa and Julie from Toast last year by Marc Zornes, an expert in food-waste reduction, and I was so excited to learn that they treat waste as a resource *instead* of a problem. In a nutshell, Toast receives surplus bread from several bakeries and sandwich-makers, which they then add to their beer, making a variety of lagers and ales that are not only good for the planet but also taste delicious.

They have very kindly let us include their home-brew recipe here, so that you can have a go at using leftover bread to make beer too. The process is no different to standard brewing, except that bread is used to replace a third of the grains. The bread is combined with malted barley in hot water and naturally occurring enzymes in the malt turn the starch into sugar, then the yeast converts the sugar to alcohol. Hops are added to give bitter flavours and aromas, and to help preserve the beer.

If you haven't tried brewing before, it's worth investing in a mash tun – you want one that will hold 26½ litres (26½ quarts). All the equipment and ingredients you'll need are available from online home-brewing suppliers. Keep the same open mind as when you make bread: some trial and error might be involved before you discover the equation of ingredients, environment and timing that gives you the desired result.

For more information about Toast, see toastale.com. And I'd also like to say a huge thanks to Rob, Louisa and Julie at Toast, long may your great work continue! **EH**

>>

Makes about 20 litres (20 quarts)

Equipment
digital thermometer
26½-litre (26½-quart) mash tun
30-litre (30-quart) pan or
    beer kettle
fermentation bucket with lid,
    airlock and siphon, tubing for
    siphoning and filling bottles,
    sterilised
about 20 empty 1-litre (1-quart)
    bottles and lids, sterilised

Ingredients
Grains
3½kg (7lb 11oz) Pale Malt
1½kg (3lb 5oz) very stale bread
150g (5oz) CaraMalt
150g (5oz) Munich Malt
500g (1lb 2oz) Oat Husks

Hops
1 teaspoon German Hallertau
    Tradition
1 teaspoon Protofloc (or Irish
    Moss) fining agent
100g (3½oz) Cascade
20g (²/₃oz) Centennial
60g (2oz) Bramling Cross

Yeast
1 sachet (11½g) of Safale US-05
    ale yeast

Stage 1 – Mash
Steep all the grains in 15¾ litres
(15¾ quarts) of water at 67°C (153°F)
in your mash tun and mix. Cover and
leave for 60 minutes.

Ensure the necessary equipment is
sterilised. Only the equipment after the
wort is boiled will need sterilising. The
best way to do this is to liberally douse
the equipment in boiling water and
leave to air-dry in a clean, dry place.
The bottles can alternatively be placed
in a dishwasher.

Stage 1 – Lauter and Sparge
Simultaneously drain the liquid from
the bottom of the mash tun ('lautering')
while sluicing ('sparging') the grains
with 78°C (172°F) water from the top
to extract additional sugars. Sparge
using a watering can or colander so
that the water is distributed in a soft
spray, rather than the gush of a hose;
pouring the water over the back of a
spoon also works. Don't be tempted to
force the liquid through the wet grains,
as this may create unwanted tannin
tastes. Stop when you have 25 litres
(25 quarts) liquid ('wort') in the mash
tun – you should end up using about
20 litres (20 quarts) of water.

Stage 3 – Boil and Add Hops
Transfer the wort to your pan or beer
kettle and bring it to the boil. Add the
German Hallertau Tradition hops as
soon as it starts boiling and set a timer
for 90 minutes. (German Hallertau
Tradition hops are the 'bittering' hops
that give Toast its lip-smacking bitter
taste.) At 15 minutes to go (after
75 minutes of boiling), add the
Protofloc, which makes a clearer,

brighter-tasting wort. At 5 minutes
to go (after 85 minutes), add 15g
(½oz) Cascade hops and 10g (⅓oz)
Centennial hops. As you take the wort
off the boil (at the 90-minute mark),
add 25g (1oz) Cascade, 10g (⅓oz)
Centennial and 25g (¾oz) Bramling
Cross. (These are the aromatic hops
that add a fruity, refreshing punch to
Toast ale.)

**Stage 4 – Cool, Ferment
and Condition**
Carefully pour the wort into your
fermentation bucket, then cool it to
20°C (68°F). You can use an ice bucket
to speed this up, if you like – but be
careful not to let any unboiled water
get into your wort, which has been
sterilised by boiling. Then add the yeast
and leave to ferment. Try to keep your
wort at around 18°C (64°F) for
7 days. After 5 days, add another 60g
(2oz) Cascade hops and 35g (1¼oz)
Bramling Cross hops. Siphon the
beer into sterilised bottles, primed for
carbonation – never pour your beer
into the bottles as this introduces
oxygen that will spoil the beer. Seal the
bottles and leave in a cool, dark place
(around 12°C/54°F) for two weeks.
This secondary fermentation adds fizz
to the beer and allows it to condition
nicely. When ready, cautiously open
a bottle and enjoy!

Since bread is the second most wasted food in Europe (the first is potatoes), it makes sense to do something with the leftovers.

Buttermilk Scones

My grandma on my dad's side taught me how to pickle cabbage, onions and tend to the allotment. My grandma on my mum's side – I'm sure like many of the best grandmas – taught me how to bake. My other grandma… just kidding!

My mum's mum is still baking in her 90th year and is the best baker in all of the land, her sponge cakes, trifles and mousses are irresistible, but my main go-to is always the scone. When freshly baked these are so tempting either generously buttered or smothered in cream and homemade jam. **GH**

Makes 6 large, or 10 small

Ingredients
250g (9oz) self-raising flour, extra for dusting
1 teaspoon baking powder (baking soda)
50g (1¾oz) caster (superfine) sugar
pinch of salt
60g (2oz) cold butter, diced
1 large egg, lightly beaten
50ml (1¾fl oz) buttermilk
milk, to glaze
butter, jam and clotted cream, to serve

Preheat the oven to 180°C (350°F) and line a large baking tray with baking paper.

Put the flour, baking powder, sugar and salt into a large bowl. Add the butter and rub it into the flour using your thumbs and fingertips, trying not to get it on the palms of your hands. (If the mixture gets too warm, it will become tough, so the idea is to use the coolest parts of your hands to do this.)

When the mixture resembles breadcrumbs, add the egg and buttermilk, then gather into a ball and turn out onto a floured work surface.

Knead the dough quickly and gently, then pat the dough out to 2½cm (1in) thick and cut into circles with a cookie cutter about 5cm (2in) wide (or use a glass if you don't have a cutter).

Transfer the scones to the baking tray, brush the tops with milk, then bake for 10–15 minutes until well-risen and light golden.

Leave to cool slightly, before serving warm with butter or cream and jam – and a good strong cup of tea.

Spelt Buttermilk Pancakes

On my very few days off from the bakery, I get intense urges to indulge, which usually materialise in the form of delicious and monstrous breakfasts. After working hard all week there are few things more satisfying than treating yourself on the morn of your rest day with something exquisitely sweet, salty and buttery. This is a favourite of ours when we're feeling especially naughty. **RS**

Makes 4–6 pancakes

Ingredients
large knob of butter, plus extra
    for frying
300ml (10½fl oz) buttermilk
275g (10oz) plain (all-purpose)
    white spelt flour
2 large eggs
2 tablespoons baking powder
¼ teaspoon sea salt
1 tablespoon caster (superfine)
    sugar
berries and crisp smoked
    streaky bacon, to serve

Melt the knob of butter in a small saucepan and set aside to cool.

Meanwhile, whisk the rest of the ingredients (except the berries and bacon) in a large bowl until there are no dry lumps of flour. Add the cooled melted butter to the batter and mix until fully incorporated.

Leave the batter to rest for 10 minutes. Do not skip this step. During the rest period, the batter will thicken and rise slightly, and the end result is a lighter, fluffier pancake.

Preheat the oven to 120°C (250°F).

Place a non-stick frying pan over a medium-high heat. Add a dollop of butter and melt until it's foaming. If you're using a small pan, add a ladleful of batter to the hot pan. If you're using a large pan, you can probably squeeze in 2 pancakes, if you don't mind odd shapes. Personally, I like non-uniform.

Fry the pancake(s) until bubbly, and almost crumpety in texture, about 1 minute. Flip and fry on the other side until the edges are dark golden and crispy, about another minute. Transfer to a plate and keep warm in the oven. Repeat until all the batter is used up.

Serve with berries and smoked streaky bacon. Sunday-morning perfection.

Buttermilk & Marmalade Gelato

Buttermilk seems like a natural addition to this gelato, partly because the citrus acidity of buttermilk pairs beautifully with tangy marmalade, and partly because after a visit to Grant's farm we came away with six litres of buttermilk, which is more buttermilk than anyone knows what to do with. My efforts to avoid food waste proved successful, and I'm excited to share this gelato with you. **EH**

Makes 500ml (17fl oz)

Ingredients
150ml (5fl oz) buttermilk
150ml (5fl oz) double
   (thick) cream
4 egg yolks
50g (1¾oz) caster (superfine)
   sugar
¾ teaspoon vanilla extract
125g (4½oz) thick-cut Seville
   orange marmalade, extra
   to serve
2 slices of stale rye bread
knob of butter
2 tablespoons candied mixed
   peel (optional)
pinch of sea salt

If you don't have an ice-cream maker, hand-churn the mixture by taking it out of the freezer and running a fork through it every 30 minutes for 2 hours – and then, when it's too solid to fork, folding it with a spoon until it resembles gelato.

Gently heat the buttermilk and cream in a medium saucepan over a medium heat. Meanwhile, whisk together the egg yolks, sugar, vanilla and marmalade in a large glass bowl.

When the buttermilk mixture is steaming but not boiling, begin whisking the egg mixture once more and pour in a splash of the buttermilk mixture. Keep whisking as you gradually add the buttermilk mixture – go slowly, so as not to cook the egg and curdle the custard.

Pour the custard back into the saucepan and cook over a medium heat for 8–10 minutes: it should thicken slightly but still be runny. Be careful not to let the custard boil, or the proteins that give the gelato its gooey texture will be broken down. Let the custard cool to room temperature before covering with plastic wrap/clingfilm and chilling it in the fridge for 4 hours, or preferably overnight.

Next, make the candied rye topping. Pulse the rye bread to chunky breadcrumbs in a food processor. Melt the butter in a large frying pan on a medium-high heat and add the breadcrumbs in a single layer (if your frying pan is too small, you'll have to do this in batches). It's best not to stir the breadcrumbs for 5 minutes, then stir every now and again until they release their natural sugars and become sticky and a little crunchy. Remove from the heat and leave to cool.

When you're ready to churn, add the custard to your ice-cream maker and churn as per the instructions. You can add some candied peel if you like. Bear in mind that its low sugar content might mean the gelato won't go completely stiff; if this happens, churn it for 20 minutes and then freeze to solidify it.

Serve with a dollop of marmalade and a sprinkling of candied rye.

Buttermilk Tart

The best shortcrust pastry is minimally worked and well rested, creating the most crumbly delicious case for a pie or tart. **GH**

Serves 10–12

Ingredients
150g (5oz) granulated sugar
10g (½oz) cornflour (cornstarch)
¾ teaspoon sea salt
5 eggs
400ml (13fl oz) buttermilk
60ml (2fl oz) double (thick) cream
55g (2oz) butter, melted, extra for greasing
1½ teaspoons vanilla extract
grated zest and juice of 1 lemon
2 tablespoons caster (superfine) sugar
fresh peaches or berry compote, to serve

For the pastry
200g (7oz) plain (all-purpose) flour
1 tablespoon caster (superfine) sugar
½ teaspoon sea salt
150g (5½oz) cold butter, diced, extra for greasing
1 large egg, separated, for the dough
1 egg, separated, for the egg wash
about 1 tablespoon chilled water

Start by making the pastry. Put the flour, sugar and salt into a food processor and whizz together. Add the butter and pulse until the mixture resembles breadcrumbs. Add 1 egg white (reserving the yolk). Add the water and pulse to form a dough. If the mixture seems too dry, gradually add a few more drops of water, pulsing each time and adding just enough to bring the dough together.

Shape the dough into a ball, wrap tightly in plastic wrap/clingfilm and leave to rest in the fridge for at least 4 hours, or up to 2 days. When ready, remove the dough from the fridge and leave to stand at room temperature for 30 minutes.

Grease a 30cm (12in) tart tin with a removable base. Lightly flour your work surface and roll out the dough big enough to fill the tin with overhang. Ease the pastry circle into the tin, carefully pressing it into the sides – don't worry about any pastry overhang as this can be trimmed later. Chill in the fridge for 30 minutes.

Preheat the oven to 185°C (365°F). Line the tart case with baking paper and fill with baking beans or uncooked rice, then blind-bake for 20–25 minutes, or until the pastry is golden brown.

Remove the paper and beans. Brush the pastry with the other egg white to seal it (reserve the yolk). Bake the tart case for a further 5 minutes. Remove the tart case, then reduce the oven temperature to 150°C (300°F). Let the tart case cool slightly, then use a sharp knife to carefully trim the overhanging edges.

Next, make the filling. In a large bowl, mix together the sugar, cornflour and salt. Separate 5 eggs, then add all the yolks together with the 2 reserved egg yolks, to the bowl. Beat thoroughly to combine. Add the lemon zest and juice, buttermilk, cream, butter and vanilla, and whisk everything together well.

Pour the mixture into the warm tart case, filling it to just shy of the rim, then bake for 20 minutes. Sprinkle the caster sugar across the top and bake for a further 20 minutes until the centre wobbles only very slightly when the tart is jiggled.

Take the tart out of the oven and blast with a blow-torch – or under a hot grill – until the sugar is caramelised. When cool to handle, remove the tart from the tin and transfer to a wire rack to cool for 2 hours. Chill in fridge for another 2 hours.

Set Buttermilk

This dessert is very similar to regular panna cotta, but as the main ingredient is buttermilk instead of cream, it's lighter with a delicious acidity. In my opinion, this makes it a much better summertime dessert, because it doesn't leave you feeling too sticky in the heat.

You can either use small moulds or one large one – you'll just need to be more patient when it comes to waiting for the larger one to set. In any case, the buttermilk will take several hours to set, so it's best to make this dessert the day before. I tend towards the smaller individual bowls, or make and serve them in glasses alongside a sticky plum and port sauce or a scattering of candied nuts, or simply with some fresh fruit. **GH**

Makes 6 individual desserts, or 1 large dessert

Ingredients
1 vanilla pod (bean)
200ml (7fl oz) good quality whole milk
250g (9oz) caster (superfine) sugar
6 gelatine leaves
800ml (27fl oz) buttermilk
fruit (such as salted plum jam and a generous dash of port), or candied nuts, to serve

Split the vanilla pod in half with a sharp knife. Scrape out the seeds and set aside for later.

Pour the milk into a large saucepan, then add the vanilla pod and the sugar. Bring to a simmer, then take off the heat.

Soak the gelatine according to the packet instructions, then squeeze out any excess liquid and add to the hot milk. Stir until the gelatine has completely dissolved.

When the milk mixture is lukewarm, whisk in the buttermilk, then pour the mixture into a jug through a fine sieve.

Stir in the reserved vanilla seeds, then pour into eight 150ml (5fl oz) moulds or one large 1½-litre (1½-quart) mould. Refrigerate until set, about 4 hours.

Serve with your topping of choice – and maybe a glass of dessert wine, such as orange muscat or Sauternes.

Index

Acknowledgements

We'd first like to thank the super team behind the creation of the book: designer, Gemma, photographer, Patsy, stylist, Linda. Thanks to Alison, Kathy and Vanessa for their help with the text and index. We'd like to especially thank Zena for taking a risk on us as new writers and being so kind and understanding throughout the whole process – thank you for helping us fulfil a lifelong ambition, we don't say this lightly!

Richard Snapes

Mum and Dad for giving me an incredible childhood, always believing in whatever I'm up to, and always being there when I'm having a meltdown.

My brother and sister Dan and Lauren for making extra effort to see me at the bakery and introducing your kids to real bread. My granny Joan for giving me my first memory of home-baked bread and being a creative inspiration.

Meagan Bennell who was there at beginning of The Snapery and continues to be an inspiration and a great friend. Phillip Clayton at Haxby Bakehouse for being my mentor and trouble-shooting bakery guru. Adam Sellar (formerly of The Little Bread Pedler) for being an inspiration: your bread was the first memorable bread I ate after moving to London – I'll never forget it. Brett Rollings for being a patient chef and paving my way in food. Olia Hercules (who is responsible for my starter) for being a wonderful friend, giving great writing advice and always believing in my bread and showcasing it in your first book. Zac and Chuse at Bar Tozino for being my very first customers. Those first baguettes were not pretty, so thanks for sticking by me! Roland and all at The Watchhouse coffee shops, you guys were one of my first customers, we've grown up together and now we're great business buddies.

The Snapery Bakery bakers past and present: Louise Bannon. Shay Briscoe. Anna Choonpicharn. Cindy Zurias. George Cavendish. Ben Lines, whose pioneering flavour combinations are a constant source of delight – we're still yet to see the 'Banana miso sourdough' though!… Thanks for all the delicious breakfasts. Lauren Duncan who changed the way we shape on her trial shift. James Whittaker, who is a longstanding member: you plough through any work load like it's no big deal, and you crack me up constantly. Alysha Aggarwal, you've stuck with me for over 2 years and have become an excellent friend, always with such perfect advice when I need an ear. Thanks for putting up with my crap! Willem Harvey, your commitment astonishes me. You've never let us down, one Christmas working for three weeks without a day off with me – we nearly went insane but we got through it. Big thanks for giving my business an actual structure.

Thanks to all my amazing friends and family who have suffered a little from my lack of presence during the process of building a business. I'd say I'm about 30 years off retiring, so we can hang out then.

Finally, the one, the only Eve Hemingway. You're the one that stops me going insane. When I go crazy, you bring me back to reality. Life seems easier when I'm with you. You have a huge talent in writing and I can't wait to see what you do. You're a genius, I love you.

Grant Harrington

I feel outstandingly lucky to have had my mum and dad support me through every step of my butter journey, it goes without saying I wouldn't be here if it wasn't for you, obviously (dad joke!). But I can't thank you enough for all the hours of physical work, presents, presence and love I get from you. Mum, to this day you consistently drive up to Nottingham to deliver butter to Sat Bains, while Dad burrows away on Excel with my accounts.

Kirk and Bryony, my brother and sister-in-law, who have made dozens of buttermilk tarts. Your supportive business advice is endlessly helpful. Also, my promise to cook at your beautiful farm wedding set me on this butter journey.

Tim and Alison and all the Malins, for putting up with me as a messy farm lodger – I know I make a cacophony of butter-making noises, often through the night and early mornings, and Bobby is the world's loudest barker! Thanks for letting me build a cabin on your farm and for letting me borrow your legendary farm electrician 'scrap' to rewire the industrial three-phase back to my cabin.

Uncle Graham and all the Stanleys, again, butter wouldn't be made without you, my main electrician, fixer and mechanic. Despite being a fair drive away, you are constantly here if I ever need something fixing. And thanks to great friend Jake Croft who helped install all the electrics.

Thanks grandma Thelma for all the baking inspiration and support!

A two Michelin-starred chef's opinion on seasoning in the food industry was critically important to a young producer starting out, as one of my first customers, thanks to Sat Bains for helping to guide the way in the simplest yet insanely important attention to salt. While working under Magnus Nilsson, I witnessed every aspect of attention it was possible to place on each ingredient used: it was this essence of appreciation that electrified my passion for butter. Professionals and friends in the industry with endless knowledge and help from Dr Johnny Drain, chief fermenting whizz, to my old director of logistics Carl Wicklund, who entrusted me as an executive of logistic our in France, helping me earn a little to help fund my butter journey.

Sarah, you are all I could have wished for. You turn up and help on the days that I have an insane amount of butter to deal with and you are the biggest moral support to slap me in the face. You are my rock to escape to, lean on and to learn with.

Fiona and Keith Watson, for letting me churn butter on their sailboat Jay Jay!

Eve and Richard for helping put pen to paper with this book and for our shared joy in bread and butter! Finally, Bobby my dog, for keeping my tail wagging.

Eve Hemingway

I'd of course like to thank my mum, Janet and my dad, Clive. Thanks as well to Auntie Jane for posting me snippets from food magazines over the years. Thanks to my lovely friends for eating and testing the delicious and not so delicious creations and for always believing I'd write about food and never being surprised by my madness: Sam, Hannah, Gabriel, Rebecca, Maud, Aiden, Phoebe, Hanna, Arabella, Rhe, Roz, Ro, Mano, Annie, Vicky, Mari and Tom. I'd like to thank the professors who let me write about food throughout my studies, namely Gordon McMullan, Clare Brant, Janet Floyd and Bridget Conor. And the teachers from school who nurtured my creative streak, Nicky Archer and Jenny Whitehead. I'd also like to mention some important people from my professional sphere: Charu Murthy for being so understanding when I couldn't work in the corporate world any longer. Thanks to Marc and Giles from Winnow and Michael-George from Plumen, for facilitating flexible working that gave me the space to write. I'd like to thank Olia for giving us a push to submit our proposal and my coach, Beth, for making scary things less scary. Penultimate in this long list, I'd like to thank Grant for all the buttery goodness and kind words about my work. Lastly, I'd like to thank Rich, for his ceaseless faith, support, love and dinners.

Thanks to the following talented makers for lending their beautiful wares during the photo shoots:

Kitchen Provisions
kitchenprovisions.co.uk

Grain & Knot
grainandknot.com

Slow Split
slowsplit.com

Cath Pots
instagram.com/cathpotsss

Lazy Eye Ceramics
lazyeyeceramics.com

Aiden China
facebook.com/aidenchinaceramics

Sources used in the research of this book:

Bread: A Global History, William Rubel, Reaktion Books, London, 2015

Bread: A Slice of History, Marchant, Reuben & Alcock, The History Press, Gloucestershire, 2010

Bread, Scott Cutler Shershow, Bloomsbury, London and New York, 2016

The History of Bread: from Pre-historic to Modern Times, John Ashton, Brooke House Publishing Co, London, publication date unknown [circa 1904]

Bread is Gold, Massimo Bottura and Friends, Phaidon, London, 2017

The Tivoli Road Baker, Michael and Pippa James, Hardie Grant Books, Melbourne, 2017

Tartine Bread, Chad Robertson, Chronicle Books LLC, 2013

Six Thousand Years of Bread: Its Holy and Unholy History, H. E. Jacob, Skyhorse Publishing, New York, 2014

Butter: A Rich History, Elain Khosrova, Algonquin Books of Chapel Hill, North Carolina, 2016

Butter and Margarine, Lorna Hinds, Franklin Watts Ltd., London, 1977

A Little Bit of Butter, Cork Butter Museum, 2007

Butter & Cheese Making, V. Cheke and A. Sheppard, Granada Publishing Ltd. 1980

Home-made Butter, Cheese and Yogurt, Maggie Black, EP Publishing Ltd. 1977

All About Butter, Butter Council leaflet, 1993

The Well-Kept Kitchen, Gervase Markham, Penguin, London, 2011

The Book Nobody Read: Chasing the Revolutions of Nicolaus Copernicus, Owen Gingerich, Walker, New York, 2004

The lake dwellings of Switzerland and other parts of Europe, Ferdinand Keller, Longman, Greens & Co., London, 1878

A Natural History of Domesticated Mammals, Juliet Clutton-Brock, Cambridge University Press, Cambridge, 1999

'Botteghe Storiche: A Study of the Disappearance of Historic Food Shops and Its Role in the Transformation of Rome's Urban Social Life', Sonia Massari, Elena T Carbone and Salem Paulos.pp153-168 in *Urban Foodways and Communication: Ethnographic Studies in Intangible Cultural Food Heritages Around the Globe*, ed. Casey Mon Kong Lum and Marc de Ferriere Le Vayer, Rowman & Littlefield, London, 2016

Culinary Jottings for Madras, Wyvern, Prospect Books, 2008

An Essay on Tea, Sugar, White Bread and Butter, Country Alehouses, Strong Beer and Geneva and other Modern Luxuries, author unknown, Salisbury, J. Hodson, 1777

The Birth of the English Kitchen: 1600–1850, Sara Pennell, Bloomsbury, London and New York, 2016

Reading Writing Recipe Books 1550–1800, ed. Michelle DiMeo and Sara Pennell, Manchester University Press, 2013

The Art of Cookery made Plain and Easy, Hannah Glasse, W. Strahan et al., London, 1774

A complete collection of genteel and ingenious conversation, according to the most polite mode and method now used at court, and in the Best Companies of England. Jonathan Swift, B. Motte, and C. Bathurst, at the Middle Temple-Gate in Fleet-Street, London, 1738

The Importance of Being Earnest, Oscar Wilde, Helicon, Dublin, 1971

Publishing Director Sarah Lavelle
Commissioning Editor Zena Alkayat
Designer Gemma Hayden
Cover Design Studio Thomas
Photographer Patricia Niven
Photographer's assistant Chris Ower
Prop Stylist Linda Berlin
Picture Researchers Liz Boyd and Sam Rolfe-Hoang
Production Director Vincent Smith
Production Controllers Stephen Lang and Jessica Otway

Published in 2018 by Quadrille, an imprint of Hardie Grant Publishing
Quadrille
52–54 Southwark Street
London SE1 1UN
quadrille.com

Text © Richard Snapes, Grant Harrington and Eve Hemingway 2018
Photography © Patricia Niven 2018
Design © Quadrille 2018

ISBN 978 1 78713 173 6

Printed in China